Sons of Sam Spade

RECOGNITIONS

Dick Riley, General Editor

detective/suspense

Ross Macdonald
By Jerry Speir

Sons of Sam Spade: The Private-Eye Novel in the 70s
By David Geherin

science fiction

Critical Encounters: Writers and Themes in Science Fiction
Edited by Dick Riley

Sons of Sam Spade

THE PRIVATE-EYE NOVEL IN THE 70s

Robert B. Parker
Roger L. Simon
Andrew Bergman

By David Geherin

Frederick Ungar Publishing Co.
New York

To Diane
and to
Christopher, Peter, and Daniel

Copyright © 1980 by Frederick Ungar Publishing Co., Inc.
Printed in the United States of America
Design by Anita Duncan

Library of Congress Cataloging in Publication Data

Geherin, David, 1943–
  Sons of Sam Spade.

  Bibliography: p.
  Includes index.
  1. Detective and mystery stories, American—History
and criticism. 2. American fiction—20th century—
History and criticism. 3. Parker, Robert B., 1932–
—Criticism and interpretation. 4. Simon, Roger
Lichtenberg—Criticism and interpretation. 5. Bergman,
Andrew—Criticism and interpretation. I. Title.
PS374.D4G4   813'.0872   79–4823
ISBN 0–8044–2231–1

Contents

Acknowledgments

I am grateful for the generous cooperation of Robert Parker, Roger Simon, and Andrew Bergman in answering questions about their work. Roger Simon also graciously provided me with a manuscript copy of *Peking Duck*. I would also like to thank my editor, Dick Riley, for his valuable suggestions and constant encouragement on this project.

D. G.

Introduction

Gumshoe. Shamus. Hawkshaw. Dick. Peeper. Snooper. Sleuth. No matter what he is called, the hard-boiled detective, or private eye, is an American institution, as native as jazz, as recognizable as Mickey Mouse, as appealing as apple pie, as durable as the game of baseball. Cloaked in many disguises and popularized through a variety of media—pulp magazines, novels, radio dramas, films, television series—he has become one of the most familiar figures in American cultural mythology.

His ancestry can be traced to private detective Race Williams, created by Carroll John Daly in a story entitled "Knights of the Open Palm," published in the June 1, 1923 issue of *Black Mask* magazine (although his prototype can be found in nineteenth-century American literature, notably in James Fenimore Cooper's *Leather-Stocking Tales* in the character of Natty Bumppo). Four months later, Dashiell Hammett introduced the Continental Op in *Black Mask*, and for the next decade, in the figure of the Op and, more importantly, in the character of Sam Spade in *The Maltese Falcon*, he gave shape to the image of the tough, cynical detective that was to serve as the model for all later private eyes. Hammett was followed by Raymond Chandler, who began contributing to *Black Mask* in 1933; from his first novel, *The Big Sleep*, published in 1939, until his last, *Playback*, in 1959, Chandler's character of Philip Marlowe broadened the outlines of Hammett's hero and brought new popularity to the hard-boiled detective novel. Then came Ross Macdonald who, in the three decades since Lew Archer's initial appearance in *The Moving Target* in 1949, has become the dominant writer in the genre, enjoying enormous critical and popular success. These three were certainly not the only writers of detective fiction.

1

However, their contributions have been so significant, their influence so pervasive, their heroes so well known, that when one thinks of the private detective, one automatically thinks of Sam Spade, Philip Marlowe, and Lew Archer, whose names are virtually synonymous with the popular image of the private eye.

Since Chandler's death in 1959, Ross Macdonald has almost had the field to himself as the unchallenged master of the form. But Lew Archer won't live forever, and the question arises whether the tradition of the hard-boiled novel is moribund, having reached its apex with Macdonald. Is the private eye, one might ask, actually a creature of the past, an anachronistic hero who is kept alive, well beyond his normal life span, by the singular efforts of Ross Macdonald? Or is the figure of the private eye perhaps so closely identified with Sam Spade, Philip Marlowe, and Lew Archer that younger writers are scared away by fears that there is nothing significantly new to be added to the dimensions of the character? Happily, on the basis of the evidence in recent years, the answer to all of the above questions is a resounding no. The emergence of several talented writers in the seventies offers clear and ample evidence that the private eye is very much alive, the hard-boiled genre still viable and open to creative innovation. The ten novels examined in the following pages, all published since 1973, bear witness to a healthy and vigorous renewal of the form.

Budding writers of private-eye novels are like salmon who swim blindly against the tide of success in their instinctive desire to return to the source for inspiration for their own creative efforts. Only the hardiest, most talented, and most inventive are able to establish their own identities and escape the common fate of dying out after producing but a single novel. Within the past decade, however, at least three writers have emerged who can lay claim to serious consideration as fourth-generation successors to their preeminent forebears. The three—Robert B. Parker, Roger L. Simon, and Andrew Bergman—also illustrate in their works differing ways of approaching a tradition whose development over the past fifty years has been largely dominated by the contributions of only three writers.

Like Chandler and Macdonald, both of whom realized that simple imitation of their predecessors was not enough, these fourth-generation writers well understand that the key to success is developing a unique approach, one that combines respectful adherence to the conventions of the genre with their own individual talents and fictional concerns. Parker, for example, hews closely to the tradition by creating a modern hero, Spenser, who combines the best features of Marlowe and Archer. Simon, on the other hand, is more innovative, incorporating the traditional qualities of the hero in a contemporary detective, Moses Wine, whose background and experiences differ significantly from those of most of his fictional colleagues. Bergman's technique approaches parody as he imitates the style of the classic hard-boiled novel and places his hero, Jack LeVine, in a series of adventures actually set in the forties. These three sons of Sam Spade—Spenser, Moses Wine, and Jack LeVine—are the new breed, the fresh faces that are giving new life to the hard-boiled novel in the seventies.

One of the most significant features of the private-eye novel is its flexibility in accommodating a variety of diverse interests and approaches: Hammett, for example, began writing hard-boiled fiction in order to record his experiences as a Pinkerton detective on paper; Chandler, a middle-aged oil company executive, was attracted to the form by the opportunity he saw for experimentation with the stylistic possibilities of the American language; Macdonald, a Ph.D. in English literature, developed an effective way of combining myth, poetry, and psychology into symbolic investigations of the past. The same can be said of the latest generation of writers: Parker, until recently a professor of English, began with an academic interest in the genre and writes within the American literary tradition; Simon, an admitted Marxist, saw an opportunity to comment on contemporary American political issues; Bergman, a trained historian, found an effective vehicle for re-creating incidents from a previous era. Like their predecessors, each was drawn to something more than the simple mystery element: to the distinctive narrative style of the genre, for example, or to its effectiveness in commenting on American life, manners, morals, values, and institutions. But the primary attraction for them, as it has been for virtually all writers in the field, is the appealing figure of the detective hero, the urban cowboy fighting society's wrongs, the knight errant defending the weak and powerless against the evils of the modern city.

The private eye has from his inception been a fantasy figure, an imaginative projection of those honorable qualities—courage, strength, toughness, integrity, loyalty, incorruptibility, rugged individualism—traditionally associated with the American hero. But beginning with Chandler, there has emerged a divergent, but no less important, strain in his character, one distinguished by such traits as compassion, pity, empathy, ethical sensitivity, and self-reflection. As this duality has developed, the hard-boiled hero has undergone a significant transformation, and when one reviews the half century of his existence, a progressive softening of his character can be traced as he becomes more complex, more humanized, more vulnerable. Although Parker, Simon, and Bergman differ in many ways from one another, they all share in common this perception of the private detective as a tough guy with a poet's sensitivity, a hero with a healthy dose of humanity. Their novels celebrate both aspects of his personality, and their success in creating fresh and credible versions of the perennial private detective demonstrates that although life-styles, literary fashions, social attitudes, and political issues may have changed dramatically since his debut, the private eye exercises, and will continue to exercise, the same powerful hold on the contemporary reader's imagination as he did for readers of *Black Mask* more than fifty years ago.

One note of caution. In order to discuss fully the novels that follow, it has been necessary to include summaries of the plots. Thus, in many instances, the identity of the culprit is revealed and certain plot surprises are unavoidably given away. However, since "whodunit" is normally not the central element in hard-boiled fiction, the author hopes that readers' enjoyment of the novels will not be lessened by prior knowledge of their outcome.

1

Robert B. Parker

Robert Brown Parker was born September 17, 1932 in Springfield, Massachusetts, the son of Carroll, a telephone company executive, and Mary Pauline Parker. He attended Colby College in Waterville, Maine, graduating with a degree in English in 1954. He then joined the Army and served a tour of duty with the infantry in Korea. After completing his service, on August 26, 1956, he married Joan Hall, whom he met while both were students at Colby. He also undertook graduate study in English at Boston University, where he received his M.A. in 1957.

Parker worked at a variety of jobs for the next five years: management trainee for Curtiss-Wright Aircraft; technical writer for the Raytheon Corporation; copy writer and editor for the Prudential Insurance Company; and, for a while, executive in his own advertising agency. In 1962, with the encouragement of his wife, he returned to Boston University for his Ph.D. with the hope of becoming a college professor so that he would have more time to write, something he was finding difficult to do while working full time. Between 1964 and 1968, he taught English at Massachusetts State College, Lowell, at Suffolk University, and at Massachusetts State College, Bridgewater. In 1968, he joined the faculty at Northeastern University as an Assistant Professor of English and continued teaching there until his retirement in 1978. Parker received his Ph.D. from Boston University in 1971.

His wife, Joan, has a Masters of Education degree in Early Childhood Education and Guidance from Tufts University. She has taught at Endicott College, and is now an Educational Specialist for the Northeast Region of the Massachusetts Department of Education. The Parkers have two sons, David, born in 1959, and Daniel, in 1963, and have lived since 1959 in Lynnfield, Massachusetts.

Parker's interest in detective fiction began early. At the age of fourteen he read a mystery novel entitled *Mr. Marlow Stops for Brandy* by John Bentley and, after searching for another novel about Mr. Marlow, stumbled onto Raymond Chandler's *The Big Sleep*, which he remembers as the most exciting reading event of his youth. His professional career in detective fiction began twenty-five years later with the writing of his doctoral dissertation at Boston University, "The Violent Hero, Wilderness Heritage and Urban Reality: A Study of the Private Eye in the Novels of Dashiell Hammett, Raymond Chandler, and Ross Macdonald." In his dissertation he examines the conflict frequently dramatized in American literature between the opposing values of wilderness and civilization. Beginning with James Fenimore Cooper's portrayal of the American wilderness as a place of refuge from civilization for Natty Bumppo, Parker traces the changing role of wilderness as fact and metaphor in the works of such writers as Thoreau, Melville, Twain, Faulkner, and Hemingway. His thesis is that as progress continued in America, wilderness disappeared so that the American heroes who were once able to test their virtues in the wilderness, were eventually forced to do so in civilization.

Parker examines the heroes of the hard-boiled tradition—notably Sam Spade, the Continental Op, Philip Marlowe, and Lew Archer—as modern embodiments of the Deerslayer archetype that has its roots in nineteenth-century American literature and legend. There is one significant difference, however, between the private eye and his early forebears: with the wilderness gone, (the modern hero must either adapt to the values of civilization (which are often portrayed as corrupting), or oppose them privately with his morality.) Those virtues once required for survival in the wilderness—strength, courage, steadfastness, resourcefulness, endurance—are now needed by the modern private eye to oppose the evils of civilization. The history of the private eye is the story of the conflict between his virtue and the pervasive corruption of his society; whatever success he achieves comes less from reforming society (which resists reformation) than from avoiding corruption and preserving his own honor and integrity. Parker's thesis reminds us of the long tradition that produced the American hard-boiled hero.

It also serves as an excellent introduction to Parker's own fiction, for it reveals his thorough knowledge of the two influences—the American literary tradition and the tradition of the hard-boiled novel—which have profoundly affected his own work.

Parker put his knowledge of the hard-boiled tradition into practice following the completion of his dissertation by writing *The Godwulf Manuscript*, which he began in 1971. He admits that he wrote the novel, at least in part, because Chandler was dead; he wanted another Philip Marlowe, and so created Spenser, his own private detective.

The Godwulf Manuscript, an homage to the traditional hard-boiled novel, especially to the novels of Chandler, was published and well received in 1974. Fans of Spenser did not have to wait long for his return, for *God Save the Child* appeared later the same year. Parker's reputation has continued to grow with the publication of each new Spenser novel: *Mortal Stakes* in 1975; *Promised Land* in 1976; *The Judas Goat* in 1978. The sixth Spenser novel, *Looking for Rachael Wallace*, is scheduled to appear in 1980.

Although Parker's writing has largely been confined to the detective area, his nongenre writing reveals interests that are reflected in his mystery writing. Like his hero, Parker is a gourmet cook and for six months wrote the "Dining Out" column for *Boston* magazine. Spenser's interest in weight lifting reflects Parker's own extensive knowledge about the subject; in 1974, he published a book, *Sports Illustrated Training With Weights*, which is still widely used. But the most important of his nondetective writing is the book he wrote with his wife about her experience with breast cancer. *Three Weeks in Spring*, published in 1978, describes a period in 1975 (during Parker's writing of *Mortal Stakes*) that began with Joan Parker's unexpected discovery of a lump in her breast and ended three weeks later with her return to teaching following a mastectomy. The book is a poignant portrait of an individual as well as a family crisis, much of it written from Joan's point of view as she experiences the physical, emotional, and psychological effects arising not only from the discovery of her cancer but also from the loss of a breast. The story ends happily, not only because Joan survives her ordeal (the doctors tell her they believe they have removed all traces of the cancer), but because the Parkers emerge undefeated, having met the test before them. Parker describes their feelings by quoting

Winston Churchill's remark that: "Nothing in life is so exhilarating as to be shot at without result."

The book also provides an intimate picture of the strong and loving relationship between Bob and Joan Parker; and after reading it, one can readily see the inspiration for the character of Susan Silverman, Spenser's female companion. The affectionate and good-natured banter, the joy of shared experience and companionship, the mutual respect for each other's individuality, the softening influence of the woman on the tough guy—those qualities that characterize the relationship between the Parkers also describe that between Spenser and Susan, whose role as a humanizing influence on Spenser reflects Joan Parker's importance in her husband's life. The portrait of Bob Parker also reveals his similarity to Spenser. The hero of a novel frequently reflects his creator in some way, and a recurring hero, commonplace in detective fiction, usually reflects his creator closely. The intimate relationship between Raymond Chandler and Philip Marlowe, for example, or that between Ross Macdonald and Lew Archer, is well known. The picture one gets of Parker from *Three Weeks in Spring* confirms the suspicion that there is a good deal of him in Spenser. One learns not surprisingly that Parker, like Spenser, is a gourmet cook; that he is a large and powerfully built man who enjoys jogging and weight lifting; that he frequently quotes poetry and has a quick and irreverent wit; that he has little patience with pretentiousness; that he is sensitive, capable of responding emotionally despite the outwardly stalwart image he projects. But more than these parallel skills, interests, and personality traits, *Three Weeks in Spring* reveals something more significant—a shared perception of the nature of the world and a philosophy for dealing with its vagaries.

Two statements from the book crystalize the basic elements of this philosophy. The first expresses the view that the universe is not logically ordered: "He knew the world to be essentially haphazard and he tried hard to take it as it came." How, for example, can one logically explain something as senseless as the appearance of a lump in the breast? The second, which derives from the first, expresses a manner of responding to such unexpected occurrences: "We have to deal with what we have and not with what we fear."

Three Weeks in Spring describes the Parkers' response to a situation that demonstrates life's unpredictability; in its way, according to Parker, the book is an account of the struggle to live, in Hemingway's terms, with "grace under pressure." The essential feature of this response is that it can be applied to dramatic crises, such as the one Joan faces, to day-to-day problems, such as we all face, or to the kind of life-and-death situations that Spenser faces. Though the circumstances vary widely, the common theme in all of Parker's writing—in his dissertation, in *Three Weeks in Spring*, and in his Spenser novels—is this: one must develop a code for responding to the situations of life, and it is the quality of one's response that is the ultimate measure of character.

The growth of Parker's reputation and his success with the Spenser series enabled him to resign his professorship at Northeastern University to devote full time to writing. Parker's typical writing day begins with making breakfast, doing housework, running five miles in the morning, and writing (usually five pages a day) in the afternoon. He normally spends a month preparing a scenario and chapter outline for each book, then six months on the actual writing.

Although he plans to publish a non-Spenser novel called *Wilderness* (and thus perhaps reach an audience unfamiliar with his detective fiction), Parker has no desire to abandon his detective hero. The Spenser novels allow him the opportunity to express his ideas freely on a variety of subjects, and provide him with his greatest satisfaction as a writer.

THE GODWULF MANUSCRIPT

It should come as no surprise to a reader of *The Godwulf Manuscript* (1974) to discover striking similarities between it and the novels of Dashiell Hammett, Raymond Chandler, and Ross Macdonald, particularly when he remembers that Parker wrote his doctoral dissertation on the novels of those three writers. What is surprising, however, is the extent to which he has managed to stake out for himself an original claim to the territory already overrun by would-be successors to the three earlier masters of the hard-boiled detective novel. Parker manages the tricky task of evoking echoes of all three writers while at the same time creating a character and developing a style that are uniquely his.

The Godwulf Manuscript introduces Spenser, a thirty-seven-year-old Boston private detective. Physically fit, six-feet-one, one hundred and ninety-five pounds, an ex-heavyweight boxer who can bench press two hundred and fifty pounds ten times, Spenser is also an amateur sculptor and a gourmet cook who lavishes loving care on the preparation of food. He served in Korea (as did Parker) and is an ex-employee of the Suffolk County District Attorney's office, from which he was fired for "insubordination." He has an instinctive sense of the comic, is quick with a quip, although he frequently irritates others as a "wiseass sonuvabitch" overfond of his own wit. And he is noticeably literate; he admits to reading a lot and to having attended college, no doubt as an English major. His vocabulary is sprinkled with literary allusions (the discovery of a young girl's dead body, for example, moves him to quote from W. H. Auden's poem about the death of a youth, "Musée des Beaux Arts") and he displays a knowledge of such arcane subjects as pre-Shakespearean drama and the controversy over certain disputed words in the text of one of Hamlet's soliloquies. Moreover, the entire novel is narrated in a fresh, witty, and colorful style.

Comparisons with his predecessors—especially Sam Spade, Philip Marlowe and Lew Archer—are inevitable. Like Sam Spade, he is tough and often cynical. Like Philip Marlowe, he has a quick wit, an insolent tongue, and an observant eye for the pompous and absurd. Like Lew Archer, he frequently finds himself drawn into the personal lives of his clients. Like all three, especially Marlowe and Archer, he has a profound sympathy for life's victims and a particular fondness for the young. He has a romantic's belief in the possibility of a better world but a realist's awareness of the concrete problems of it as it is. He is a loner, preferring to follow his own private code of personal justice. A conversation between Spenser and the president of the university that hires him to solve a crime reveals his position. Spenser tells Dr. Vogel:

"The police don't belabor the obvious, Dr. Vogel. The most obvious answer is the one they like the best. Usually they're right. They don't have time to be subtle. They are very good at juggling five balls, but there are always six in the game and the more they run the farther behind they get."

"Thus you handle the difficult and intricate problems, Mr. Spenser?"

"I handle the problems I choose to; that's why I'm freelance. It gives me the luxury to worry about justice. The cops can't. All they're trying to do is keep that sixth ball in the air."

Thank God for the private eye, at least in detective fiction, for he has since his inception assumed the role of savior, defender of the weak and innocent, pursuer of truth and justice. Spenser is a full-fledged member of that honorable fraternity.

Parker also follows the example of Chandler in choosing a name for his hero that evokes memories of a more romantic age: Chandler selected Marlowe, a name with echoes of Malory, author of *Le Morte d'Arthur*, a collection of tales about King Arthur and his knights; Parker, looking to the English Renaissance, selected Spenser after Edmund Spenser, author of *The Faerie Queen*, an English heroic poem which, among other things, contains knightly adventures as well as discussions of such issues as moral behavior and the principles of personal honor. Parker said he was looking for a name that would evoke the chivalric warrior/poet/lover/fighter quality of the period, and after rejecting the name Sidney (after Sir Philip Sidney, the archetype of the Renaissance courtier), he settled on Spenser. Originally, Spenser was given the first name David, but when Parker realized that his younger son would be unhappy to discover his older brother David was being immortalized in his father's fiction, he went through the manuscript crossing out all the Davids and left Spenser without a first name.

Besides recognizing genetic similarities between Spenser and his ancestors, mystery readers will also detect echoes of the characteristic mannerisms and stylistic quirks of some notable writers of detective fiction: Hammett's hard-edged realism; Chandler's wit and irony; Macdonald's poetic images and metaphors. And yet there is more to *The Godwulf Manuscript* than a mere pastiche of literary styles, something more substantial than warmed-over Raymond

Chandler or retread Ross Macdonald. Parker introduces a private eye with enough character and style to stand on his own beside his more famous colleagues.

The novel begins with Spenser being hired to find a missing fourteenth-century manuscript that has been stolen from the rare book room of a Boston university. The manuscript is being held for a $100,000 ransom, and university officials suspect that SCACE (Student Committee Against Capitalist Exploitation), a radical campus group, is behind the attempted extortion. Spenser's investigation leads him to Terry Orchard, secretary of SCACE, and her boyfriend Dennis Powell. The case takes a tragic turn, however, when Spenser is summoned to Terry's apartment to discover that Powell has been murdered, apparently with the gun a drugged and semiconscious Terry Orchard is holding in her hand. The police refuse to believe her story that two men broke into the apartment, shot Powell with her gun, and then drugged her to make it appear that she was attempting to commit suicide. Spenser believes her and, like a genuine private eye, determines to prove her innocence.

Before long, the original case is solved when the manuscript is mysteriously returned to the university. Spenser suspects, however, that what appeared to be a simple political theft has more serious overtones. An encounter with Joe Broz, a local hoodlum, convinces him that drug peddling is involved. A second murder, that of Cathy Connelly, Terry's former roommate, provides him with the evidence he needs to uncover the truth. The trail leads to Lowell Hayden, a professor of medieval literature and campus radical who, it turns out, not only engineered the theft of the manuscript but was also involved in a campus drug ring with Dennis Powell; a disagreement with Powell over the quality of heroin the mob was supplying them led Hayden to arrange for Powell's murder. Hayden later killed Cathy Connelly to prevent her from revealing what she knew about the incident. Spenser turns Hayden over to the police and establishes Terry's innocence.

The plot, though lacking the complexity of a Ross Macdonald story, moves briskly and provides enough development to keep the reader interested. There are no real surprises or sudden revelations; the solution of the case is the result of Spenser's detective work rather than luck, intuition, or convenient confessions. For the most part, each character and scene is well integrated into the plot, and

Parker wastes little in the telling of the story. The characters are well defined, even the minor ones, notably Terry's mother, Professor Hayden's wife, Lieutenant Quirk, and Iris Milford, an editor of the campus newspaper who matches Spenser sass for sass. Parker's handling of individual scenes is outstanding, approaching Chandler at his best: the arraignment of Terry Orchard at the police station at 5:30 A.M.; a late-night encounter with Terry's mother in her lavish West Newton Hill home; the unexpected discovery of Cathy Connelly's body in her bathtub—each shows Parker's skill in developing suspense, creating atmosphere, or adding a satiric edge to the action. Parker also gives his novel a gritty sense of realism, often simply by providing a list of details: the items in a refrigerator or medicine chest; the furnishings in a house; the variety of students walking across a campus. Such details give the novel a concrete sense of place, mood, and atmosphere.

But what stands out above all else is the character of Spenser. It is in this regard that *The Godwulf Manuscript* is such an accomplishment for a first novel, for Spenser springs fully developed into the reader's imagination. By contrast, Dashiell Hammett worked for several years to evolve the character of the Continental Op, and used him in dozens of stories before he appeared in his first novel, *Red Harvest*. Raymond Chandler likewise experimented with several versions of Philip Marlowe before he presented him in his first novel, *The Big Sleep*. Even Ross Macdonald wrote stories and novels with a variety of characters before creating Lew Archer in *The Moving Target*. There are no apprentice pieces in Parker's case. Spenser's debut in *The Godwulf Manuscript* is a most auspicious one, made even more impressive by Parker's skill in presenting him to the reader as almost an old friend.

The hard-boiled detective novel has maintained its enduring popularity for more than half a century primarily because of the character of the private eye himself. In his study of the hard-boiled novel, Parker noted that: "The crime is the occasion of the story, but the subject of the story is not the detection, but the detective." The proliferation of so many private-eye series is largely due to an abiding interest in the hero himself. And what gives the hard-boiled hero his most characteristic feature is the sound of his voice. It is important to note that, with a few exceptions such as *The Maltese Falcon*, virtually every hard-boiled novel is narrated by the detective

himself and narrated *after the fact*. Hence, everything is filtered
through his consciousness and sensibility. Because of this, the reader
not only identifies readily with the hero, he often gets a revealing
insight into his character through his role as narrator. The reader
is given two important sources of information: what the hero does
(more correctly, what he says he does); and how he *tells* us what
he does. Style as well as action becomes a significant component of
the hard-boiled novel. This is not to suggest that the narrator of
the hard-boiled novel is unreliable, or distorts his role in a self-
aggrandizing way. The basic honesty of the hero is one of the conventions of the genre. But the narration of the action provides much
more than a mere summary of the events in the case; it also provides
a substantial portrait of the narrator. When the narrator speaks, he
communicates a tone, an attitude, a sensibility, even a sense of
values. The total effect is the creation of a human being with whom
the reader becomes most intimate.

What distinguishes one hard-boiled novel from another, then,
is not so much a difference in setting, theme, or plot as it is the
character of the hero and the manner in which the writer reveals
that character to the reader. Thus, Dashiell Hammett creates a
tough, highly professional Continental Op by using a tough, no-
nonsense style for his narration. Raymond Chandler characterizes a
witty but disillusioned Philip Marlowe by having him re-create his
cases in a style that is both witty in its observations and nostalgic
in its tone. Ross Macdonald reveals Lew Archer's compassion and
sympathy through his selection of carefully chosen images and
metaphors. To understand the private eye, one must pay careful
attention to the story and to what he reveals of himself in the telling
of that story.

A close examination of the opening chapter of *The Godwulf
Manuscript* illustrates Parker's skill in characterizing his hero. The
first sentence of the novel, for example, establishes not only the
setting for the action to follow but also reveals the narrator's attitude: "The office of the university president looked like the front
parlor of a successful Victorian whorehouse." We learn immediately
that the speaker has an eye for pretentious detail and an irreverent
sense of humor. When apprised of the university's precarious financial situation, Spenser suggests to the president that he rent out
the south end of his office for off-street parking. The architecture of

the campus building reminds him of the "corporate headquarters for White Tower Hamburgers." The effect of such remarks is to create a distinctive voice, that of a wise-cracking, irreverent, and witty observer. Before we know anything substantial about his character and background, we are given a distinct impression of his personality through his verbal style.

More than just a voice is revealed, however. Riding in an elevator in a classroom building, Spenser notices the omnipresent graffiti: "The elevator that took me to the fourth floor was covered with obscene graffiti that some proprietous soul had tried to doctor into acceptability, so that phrases like 'buck you' mingled with the more traditional expletives. It was a losing cause, but that didn't make it a bad one." One is reminded here of Holden Caulfield who, at the end of Salinger's *Catcher in the Rye*, expressed a similarly impossible but nonetheless chivalric desire to erase all the obscenity from the world.

This is one way Parker reminds us of the knightly role the private eye plays, a convention that derives from Chandler's portrayal of Marlowe. It is important to remember that peering over the shoulder of Spenser is his creator, Robert Parker, who is looking back over his own shoulder at the imposing figures of Hammett, Chandler, and Macdonald. In recognition of this fact, and as tribute to them, Parker uses Spenser's narrative to evoke remembrances of his antecedents. Thus he manages to place his hero in the tradition of the private eye as savior while reminding his readers of the intimate relationship between his novel and those classic novels in the hard-boiled genre.

Parker's ability to evoke specific memories of the past can be illustrated by looking at Spenser's description of a photocopy of a page from the missing Godwulf manuscript: "It showed an elegantly handwritten book lying open on a table. The words were in Latin and around the margins in bright red and gold were drawn knights and ladies and lions on their hind legs, and vines and stags and a serpentine dragon being lanced by an armor-clad hero on a plump and feminine horse." What else is this but a reminder of the private eye's role as knight errant rescuing the beautiful damsel in distress, a notion first suggested in the opening chapter of Chandler's *The Big Sleep*, when Philip Marlowe, visiting the home of General Sternwood, looks up and sees a stained-glass panel:

Over the entrance doors, which would have let in a troop of
Indian elephants, there was a broad stained-glass panel showing
a knight in dark armor rescuing a lady who was tied to a tree
and didn't have any clothes on but some very long and convenient hair. The knight had pushed the vizor of his helmet
back to be sociable, and he was fiddling with the knots on the
ropes that tied the lady to the tree and not getting anywhere.
I stood there and thought that if I lived in the house, I would
sooner or later have to climb up there and help him. He didn't
seem to be really trying.

By including his own version of the knight and his lady, Parker
accomplishes two things: he reminds the reader of the symbolic
role Spenser will play in the novel, and he pays tribute to one of the
most influential of all hard-boiled novels.

To reinforce this parallel, Parker later includes another scene
that reenacts the action described by Marlowe. Spenser learns that
Terry Orchard has left her parents' home to join a group known as
the Ceremony of Moloch. He traces their location and arrives to
find Terry naked, tied to a wooden cross, about to be initiated into
the sexual rites of the group. He dashes to her rescue, unties her, and
leads her to safety. The dramatic rescue of the beautiful and naked
damsel from the clutches of evildoers convinces us, if we had any
doubts, of the knightly role into which Spenser has been cast.

Parker makes no effort to deny his roots; on the contrary, he
takes pains to remind his readers of the debt he owes to the great
mystery writers before him. For example, a visit to the office of
gangster Joe Broz (a faint echo, perhaps, of gangster Joe Brody in
The Big Sleep), reveals it to be disguised as the Continental Con-
sulting Company, a reference perhaps to Hammett's Continental
Detective Agency. The campus security officer's secretary to whom
Spenser is attracted is Brenda Loring, a name that evokes memories
of Linda Loring, the first woman Marlowe sleeps with in The Long
Goodbye, and the woman who becomes his wife in Chandler's unfinished final novel, The Poodle Springs Story. Terry Orchard's
mother confesses to Spenser that Terry and her father do not get
along, and alludes to Mourning Becomes Electra, Eugene O'Neill's
modern version of the Greek myths, a tribute to Ross Macdonald
and his preoccupation with such Freudian themes. While none of

these allusions is intrinsic to the plot, each serves to afford faithful readers of hard-boiled novels an added pleasure.

As a writer committed to carrying on the tradition of the hard-boiled novel, Parker has to strike a delicate balance between imitation and innovation. He is nothing if not faithful to the genre; he freely uses characters, scenes, and stylistic mannerisms of his predecessors. Yet he is no slavish imitator, no hack writer with inadequate imagination, style, or creativity of his own. Another scene in the novel shows how he manages to be both imitative and original. Every hard-boiled novel contains at least one scene describing the return of the tired, lonely private eye to his shabby office. Parker obligingly includes such a scene, but re-creates it in his own style:

> One room with a desk, a file cabinet, and two chairs in case Mrs. Onassis came with her husband . . . I'd come down mainly to check my mail and the trip had been hardly worth it. There was a phone bill, a light bill, an overdue notice from the Boston Public Library, a correspondence course offering to teach me karate at home in my spare time, a letter from a former client insisting that while I had found his wife she had left again and hence he would not pay my bill, an invitation to join a vacation club, an invitation to join an automobile club, an invitation to subscribe to five magazines of my choice at once-in-a-lifetime savings, an invitation to shop the specials on pork at my local supermarket, and a number of less important letters. Nothing from Germaine Greer or Lenny Bernstein, no dinner invitations, no post cards from the Costa del Sol, no mash notes from Helen Gurley Brown. Last week had been much the same.

The whimsical descriptions, the offbeat tone, the self-deprecating attitude—these are characteristics Spenser shares with many other private detectives, but the scene is written in such a way as to give a fresh coat of paint to this battered old convention of the private eye novel.

A client who hires Spenser gets his money's worth—he gets a private detective who is tough, hard-working, dedicated to his profession and his client. One sure measure of a private eye's toughness is his tough talk; Spenser is no slouch in the mouth department and can talk as mean as the next guy. A more important measure, how-

ever, is his performance in action, and Spenser demonstrates his
strength and courage in battle. He outboxes one thug, shoots two
others in the dark after he has been wounded, and finally strangles
a giant of a man to death with his bare hands. But Parker is careful
to keep Spenser's toughness in perspective. He is clearly not interested in portraying him as a violent avenger who needs to prove
his masculinity at every opportunity, even though Spenser is an
ex-boxer and weight lifter. When he roughs up Mark Tabor, a young
student member of SCACE, in order to pry some information from
him, the youth starts to cry and Spenser consoles him: "Everyone
gets scared when they are overmatched in the dark; it's not something to be ashamed of, kid." But Tabor continues to cry and
Spenser remarks, "I had a lot of information, but I had an unpleasant taste in my mouth. Maybe on the way home I could stop
and rough up a Girl Scout." He even admits to tiring of being tough:
"Guile, I thought, guile before force. I had been thinking that more
frequently as I got up toward forty."

Spenser knows toughness alone doesn't solve cases, so he devotes a good deal of time to routine, dogged investigation. When the
police are unwilling to pursue an inquiry into Cathy Connelly's
death, preferring to consider it an accidental drowning, Spenser
breaks into her apartment and undertakes a laborious inch-by-inch
search until he finds something significant, a love letter addressed
to the dead girl. Further digging leads him to the letter writer,
Professor Lowell Hayden. He watches Hayden closely for three days,
discovering along the way new dimensions in boredom. But his
patience and hard work pay off when he finally solves the case.

Spenser's dedication arises from a variety of motives, money
not being the primary one. Like Marlowe and Archer, he is driven
by a sense of personal responsibility. On the one hand, he agrees to
work for Terry's father to prove her innocence because he believes
she is innocent and cannot bear the thought of a twenty-year-old
girl going to prison unjustly. On the other hand, his motivation is
more personal. When asked why he is so interested in Terry's case,
he answers simply, "I like her." But his dedication ultimately
transcends the personal. Even when the stolen manuscript is returned and his official role in the investigation ends, he continues.
Why? As he explains to the campus security chief, "I don't do
piecework, Tower. I take hold of one end of the thread and I keep

pulling it in till it's unraveled." His commitment is to the whole truth, not just to that part of it which he has been hired to uncover. This is why he works freelance, for he has discovered that it frees him from the two ailments that plague the police—pressure and procedure.

Pressure succeeds in scaring off the police, but not Spenser. The theft of the manuscript worries gangster Joe Broz, who fears that close investigation will expose his involvement in the campus drug scene. So he arranges to have the manuscript returned, and pressures both Spenser and the police to lay off. Captain Yates in the police department is susceptible to pressure and he responds by removing Lieutenant Quirk, a tough policeman who has earned Spenser's respect, from the case. Quirk wouldn't accept the "accidental drowning" explanation for Cathy Connelly's death, but Yates will. The police have an explanation they can make fit. But it isn't the truth and Spenser won't accept it, even though Broz has threatened him if he continues. If the police will investigate no further, then Spenser feels he must. Since the cops don't worry about justice and buckle under mob pressure, Spenser accepts the responsibility and continues the investigation on his own.

Spenser also prefers to work alone because he understands that police officers are bound by procedure. Lieutenant Quirk does not agree that the police investigation should end, but he is powerless to do anything about it. As he reminds Spenser, "One of the things that a cop has to have is discipline. He gets orders, he has to obey them or the whole thing goes to hell. I don't have to like what's happening, but I do it. And I don't run around crying about it." Spenser retorts by reminding Quirk that "It was the widely acclaimed Adolf Eichmann who popularized that 'I obey orders' routine, wasn't it?" The difference between a good cop like Quirk and a good private eye like Spenser is freedom. Spenser doesn't set himself up as another Avenger, Penetrator, Destroyer, or other typical hero of the sub-genre of revenge fiction, who works outside the law. But he does understand the limitations of the police who, out of fear, corruption, or departmental procedure, cannot pursue the thread of truth to its end as Spenser feels obliged to do.

One of the many literary allusions in the book underscores Spenser's deep sense of personal responsibility. As he leaves the hospital where he is being treated for a bullet wound, a nurse objects to his sudden departure. He responds, "You've done what you could, but I've got stuff to do and promises to keep." The allusion is to Robert Frost's "Stopping by Woods on a Snowy Evening," where the narrator is tempted to remain in the woods watching them being covered with snow one beautiful winter evening. The poem concludes with the lines, "But I have promises to keep,/And miles to go before I sleep./And miles to go before I sleep." As in Frost's poem, Spenser can't rest until he fulfills his promises, especially those made to himself. He is more than a competent professional who gives a client a good day's work for a good day's pay. He is the archetypal American hero who is blessed (sometimes cursed) with a conscience and an unswerving sense of commitment to principle. Parker well knows that the private eye has not endured all these years on toughness alone; it is the softer side of his character, his vulnerability, his humanness, which have endeared him to generations of readers. Parker humanizes his hero in subtle ways. For example, as he looks out of the police station window, Spenser sees below him a thin Puerto Rican youth dumping dirty water behind the coffee shop where he works and remarks, "I looked at my watch, 6:40. The kid had got up awful early to come in and mop the floor. I wondered how late tonight he'd be there." Nothing more need be said about the boy; Spenser's concern and sympathy for the underdog are clearly communicated. Earlier, as he walked across the university campus, he noted the sadness on the faces of the young and couldn't help empathizing with their feelings of alienation from a society which they sense has somehow let them down.

Spenser's attitude toward himself also conveys his humanness. Despite the weighty symbolic burden he has to bear as hero, knight, and savior, he never loses sight of his own weaknesses and inadequacies. He has doubts about himself: "Sometimes I wondered if I was getting too old for this work. And sometimes I thought I had gotten too old last year." He is a man who understands guilt, whether it comes from slapping a young student around or because he has made love to Mrs. Orchard, mother of the girl he is trying to save and wife of the man who has hired him. He has a big mouth and winces when he can't learn to keep it shut at appropriate times. And he has an effective ironic wit which he frequently uses for self-deflation. After an extended analysis of Mrs. Orchard's motives in asking him to put a log on the fire, he finally reaches the simple conclusion that she probably just wanted another log on the fire. His reaction: "Sometimes I'm deep as hell." Or later, when his survey of the situation tells him that the apartment he is looking for is on one floor of a building and it turns out to be on another, he says, "I was wrong. It was the third floor. Close observation is my business." This combination of toughness and vulnerability makes Spenser a very appealing character. What Philip Durham said of Philip Marlowe applies with equal merit to Spenser's character: "He was the hero that men in their feckless souls imagine themselves being; he was the hero that women in their optimistic hearts hope they have married."

One notable difference between Spenser and his predecessors concerns his private life. Even if one does not accept Ross Macdonald's argument that Lew Archer is such a thinly defined character he would disappear if he turned sideways, it is true that much of Archer's substance as a character is due simply to the fact that he has appeared in so many novels. Philip Marlowe was more fully developed as a character, for which Macdonald criticized Chandler, arguing that excessive development of the hero detracts from the rest of the novel. Yet even Marlowe's private life, what there was of it, remained private. Such is not the case with Spenser.

Spenser has many interests beyond his profession, and he has an active sexual life. There are indications that he entertains women in his apartment, and at the end of the novel he calls Brenda Loring, a woman who has excited him from the moment he first saw her wearing a dress that was "too short for a skirt and too long for a belt." He is certainly not guilty of celibacy, as Marlowe and Archer were, at least for most of their careers. When, for example, Marlowe returns to his apartment and discovers a naked Carmen Sternwood in his bed in *The Big Sleep*, he flatly rejects her invitation to join her and, until *The Long Goodbye*, refuses all other female temptations. When the naked Terry Orchard beckons Spenser to his bed (in yet another reenactment of a scene from *The Big Sleep*), Spenser doesn't hesitate for a moment. Here, and in the previous chapter where he made love to Terry's mother, Spenser is not the aggressor, nor does he use his influence to take advantage of vulnerable females. He simply responds to good old-fashioned lust, the human urge that Marlowe and Archer spent so much time and energy suppressing. Spenser's open attitude toward sexual behavior may simply be a reflection of the greater freedom in the novel today compared to the thirties and forties. But there seems to be a more significant difference, that is, a desire on Parker's part to move away from the myth of the celibate hero. In Parker's version of the private eye myth, refusal of sex is not to be taken as a measure of moral character.

The Godwulf Manuscript is not without its flaws. The resolution of the plot is too pat. The source of evil in the book turns out to be a crackpot whose misguided political idealism gets mixed up with a naïve and dangerous view of drugs as liberators of social consciousness. Parker fails to locate the evil in a larger context, neither placing it in a social frame, as Chandler does, nor in a familial one, as Macdonald does. Parker appears to be less interested in the *why* of crime than many of his predecessors were. Although most of the literary references and allusions are effective and appropriate, some, notably the many references to hell, don't work. Despite references to Dante's *Inferno*, Milton's *Paradise Lost*, and even a character modeled after Moloch, one of the fallen angels, there is no coherent attempt to relate the evil in the book to anything more significant than a demented character who gets himself involved with the mob.

Although the plot is well developed, some scenes are not effectively integrated into the novel. For example, the scene where Spenser rescues Terry Orchard from the Ceremony of Moloch seems largely designed to do two things, both of which are external to the plot: one, show Spenser reenacting the knightly role; and two, give Terry equal time, sexually speaking, with her mother, whom Spenser bedded in the previous chapter. Certain characters and relationships are also undeveloped and unresolved. Terry's father, an arrogant and overbearing character, simply disappears after hiring Spenser to prove his daughter's innocence. The potential for an interesting father-daughter conflict is there, but remains undeveloped, possibly because Parker felt he was getting too close to Ross Macdonald territory. At the end of the novel, Spenser returns Terry to her parents' door and beats a hasty retreat, leaving the reader to speculate about the nature of their reunion.

Most of these flaws can be attributed to the inexperience of a first novelist. One does not wish to carp about them too much, for they are minor when compared to the successes of the book—

Parker's skill in creating character, especially that of Spenser; his crackling dialogue; his witty and ironic observations; his clever descriptions—all wrapped up in a flashy style polished to a bright sheen. *The Godwulf Manuscript* is a remarkable first novel and a promising introduction to the series.

Despite his devotion to his models and his faithfulness to the genre of the hard-boiled novel, Parker is surprisingly successful in carving out his own individual niche. One of the most important ways he separates himself from Chandler and Macdonald is in his choice of location; Spenser's turf is Boston, a locale that, with a few exceptions, is fresh territory for the private eye. Boston cannot match the symbolic resonance of Hollywood or the satiric possibilities of the Southern California setting that has become another convention of the genre. But Boston is an urban center with its own character and potential, from the seedy decadence of the Combat Zone next to Spenser's office to the well-heeled elegance of West Newton Hill.

Rather than ending on a downbeat note as so many hard-boiled novels do, with the private eye heading off to another night of loneliness and despair, *The Godwulf Manuscript* concludes with Spenser phoning Brenda Loring and listening to her laugh, a "good laugh, full of promise." No dark night of the soul for him. The job is over. Justice has triumphed, life goes on. Spenser looks outward instead of inward.

GOD SAVE THE CHILD

There is in the sports world a term, "sophomore jinx," which is used to explain the decline in performance that often afflicts athletes after an especially outstanding rookie year. There is no such comparable term in the literary world, although the malady of diminished performance in a writer's second effort is all too common. In his second Spenser novel, *God Save the Child* (1974), Parker manages to avoid the problems of the follow-up performance, and takes a confident step forward in his development as a mystery writer. Having paid his debts to his celebrated predecessors in *The Godwulf Manuscript*, Parker moves out from under their shadow in his second novel. Of course, one cannot write a hard-boiled detective novel that is not indebted to the conventions of the genre and the influence of past masters. But Parker manages to avoid the obvious parallels he employed in *The Godwulf Manuscript*. Instead he concentrates on developing his material his own way.

The novel begins with Spenser hired to find fifteen-year-old Kevin Bartlett, an apparent runaway, who has been missing for a week. A ransom note soon arrives at the Bartlett home, and it now appears that Kevin was kidnapped. His parents agree to pay $50,000 for his return, but after the ransom is paid, several events occur: when the police arrive to pick Kevin up at the spot designated by the kidnappers, they find instead a life-sized rag doll dummy in an old hearse; Kevin's mother receives a death threat; Earl Maguire, the Bartlett family friend and lawyer, is murdered in the Bartlett house. Spenser is no longer certain whether he is looking for an innocent kidnapping victim or a cruel prankster who is implicated in a murder. He discovers the truth to be somewhere between the two extremes. He finally locates Kevin with his "kidnapper," reunites him with his parents, and solves Maguire's murder. But he also uncovers something unexpected—a drug and prostitution ring that involves some of the most respected citizens of Smithfield, the fictional Massachusetts community in which the novel is set. And before the case is over, another murder occurs, one for which Spenser himself feels responsible.

All of the qualities that distinguished *The Godwulf Manuscript* are here—clever dialogue, vivid characters, a witty narrative style, and, as compelling as ever, the character of Spenser. Furthermore, the rough edges and uncertainties of Parker's first novel have been eliminated. The plot, for example, is much more skillfully handled, more logically developed; the characters are more interesting; the excesses of Spenser's narrative have been reduced. All in all, in *God Save the Child* Parker exercises tighter control of his material than he did in his first novel.

Spenser is still the same engaging Spenser—there are no dramatic changes in his character, no previously undisclosed sides to

his personality. What Parker does, however, is soften some elements
and highlight others to give him greater depth and substance. For
example, he tones down his wisecracks, which admittedly tended to
become annoying in *The Godwulf Manuscript*. Where Spenser
strove to have the last word in every exchange in the first novel he
no longer feels compelled to demonstrate his toughness and wit by
topping every remark made to him. While there may be a certain
boyish cleverness about Spenser's quick remarks, Parker grants him
a greater degree of maturity in *God Save the Child*, though Spenser
is still far from being a sober, tight-lipped bore. One aspect of
Spenser's character more fully developed in this novel is his private
life, especially his relationship with women, or more accurately with
one woman, Susan Silverman. *The Godwulf Manuscript* established
that Spenser was no stranger to sexual encounters. Parker clearly
does not want to use sexual abstinence as a measure of his hero's
moral or professional character. But in *God Save the Child*, Spenser's
sexual activity is limited to Susan Silverman, a guidance counselor
at Kevin's school who gives Spenser professional insight into Kevin's
personality and offers possible explanations for his behavior toward
his parents. Susan is divorced, in her late thirties, with black eyes
and shoulder-length black hair. Spenser is attracted by her "intelligent maturity" and her laugh, which he describes as sounding
"like I'd always imagined the taste of mead. It was resonant."
(Spenser has a particular fascination with laughter: it was the
promising sound of Brenda Loring's laughter over the phone that
ended *The Godwulf Manuscript*; in *Mortal Stakes*, the next Spenser
novel, it is once again Susan's smile that intrigues him so, inspiring
him to rhapsodize about "that sunrise of a smile that colored her
whole face and seemed to enliven her whole body." By the time
Promised Land appears, Susan's smile has become "Technicolor,
Cinemascope and stereophonic sound.")

The wooing of Susan is handled with sensitivity and wit.
Spenser invites her to his apartment, partly to sample his pork
tenderloin *en croûte* (a potential *faux pas* when he suddenly remembers she is Jewish; she tells him she is not orthodox and not
to worry), partly for information about Kevin (which he gets), and
partly to make a pass at her (which he attempts). She is flattered
by his interest, but confesses that she is old-fashioned enough still

to adhere to her mother's warning that "only dirty girls did it on the first date." She promises to be more receptive on their next date; Spenser, suffering from a severe case of what he calls "terminal tumescence," suggests they immediately hop into his car and drive to her place for that second date. The intimacy that develops between the two arises naturally and is used by Parker to reveal a dimension to Spenser's character he would be unable to portray through his professional activities or narrative style alone. We see a man capable of responding emotionally and intellectually, and not just physically, to a beautiful woman whose intelligence and sense of humor complement his. The sexual nature of their relationship, while not unimportant, is not predominant and is allowed to develop (decorously offstage) only after a solid personal relationship has been established. And also, unlike the situation in many novels in the genre, the woman to whom the hero is attracted is neither a suspect in the case nor a threat to the performance of his duty; she is simply part of his private life. The presence of Susan gives Spenser an emotionally fulfilling relationship without the confining aspects of domesticity; Parker thus avoids the regrettable mistake of Raymond Chandler, who had Philip Marlowe marry with devastating results in his unfinished *The Poodle Springs Story*. Parker offers Spenser an emotional anchor in his life and yet gives him the needed freedom of his calling.

The disappearance of a child and the subsequent revelation that it was prompted by his search for a substitute father introduces a theme that has all but been patented by Ross Macdonald; Parker's comment in his doctoral dissertation about Macdonald's *The Instant Enemy* could well serve as an epigraph for his own novel: "Throughout the novel the cruelty and crime emerge out of mismanaged family life, through a breakdown in the relationship between parent and child." Such themes as the alienation of the young, the hostility between parent and child, the search for a substitute family structure, which were implied in *The Godwulf Manuscript*, are treated much more explicitly in *God Save the Child*. At the end of *The Godwulf Manuscript*, Spenser returned Terry Orchard to her family but left her at her parents' door, unwilling to become involved in what he dismisses as "family business." But in *God Save the Child*, Parker focuses directly on family business and develops the theme of the confused youth whose emotional crisis is precipitated by a family situation that is portrayed as being all too characteristic of modern American society.

Roger Bartlett, owner of a successful Smithfield construction company, and his attractive and stylishly dressed wife Marge, come to Spenser's office to hire him to find their missing son. In the scene that follows, Parker deftly reveals the characters of the Bartletts and exposes the conflicts that have obviously contributed to their son's disappearance. Marge Bartlett is a "modern" woman who devotes her considerable energies almost exclusively to self-expression, either through her dance, art, or sculpture classes, or through her carefully applied makeup and expensive clothes: Spenser's description of her—"Her face had a bland, spoiled, pretty look, carefully made up with eye shadow and pancake makeup and false eyelashes. She looked as though if she cried she'd erode."—exposes the artifice that explains much of her character. She tells Spenser she takes acting lessons twice a week because "I'm a very creative person, you know, and I have to express myself." When her husband scoffs at this, she reminds him that "Creative people simply must create. If you're not a creative person you wouldn't understand." Unfortunately for her, Spenser and the reader understand only too well that Marge's prattling reveals narcissism, not creativity, and exposes a self-centeredness that is shown to have damaging effects on her family. While his wife is all wrapped up in her creative pursuits, Roger works hard at his business to pay for all her activities. Consequently, he has little time for his family, which is thus left essentially parent-less. Roger is basically a decent, straightforward man who, however, is dominated by his wife and has abdicated his role as father in favor of total immersion in his work.

Before long the simmering hostility between the Bartletts spills out in Spenser's office, tarnishing the carefully cultivated image of the contemporary couple Marge is trying so hard to project. When she accuses her husband of being too cheap to pay for professional help for Kevin, he retorts by attacking her selfishness: "You bitch," he said, "I told you, take the money out of your goddamned acting lessons, and your goddamned pottery classes and your goddamned sculpturing supplies and your goddamned clothes. You got twenty years' psychology payments hanging in your goddamned closet . . ." This is only the first of several such arguments Spenser witnesses, and at times he must feel as if he has stumbled onto a performance

of Edward Albee's *Who's Afraid of Virginia Woolf.* The only difference is that in Albee's play George and Martha argue over an
imaginary child, whereas in *God Save the Child,* the child is real and
so are his problems.

The Bartletts also have a daughter, Dolly, age fourteen, and
Parker uses her to illustrate the destructive effects of the parents
on the children, the pressures that have already driven her brother
away. She wanders around the house no more noticeable to her
parents than a piece of furniture. Only when her mother doesn't wish
her to hear an unflattering or embarrassing remark does she take
note of her existence long enough to ask her to leave. Yet nothing
escapes her attention. Spenser earns her trust and learns that Marge,
according to Dolly, "screws with everybody" and that everybody
except Roger knows it (probably because he's too busy to notice).
Dolly says her mother's actions don't bother her much any more
because she has gotten used to them, but she tells Spenser that they
drove Kevin crazy. Later, when the Bartletts begin another ugly
argument, Spenser notices Dolly hurrying up the stairs to her room,
and he mutters to himself, "Pleasant dreams, kid."

As the novel continues, the portrait of Marge Bartlett becomes
more unflattering. Returning to the Bartlett house after accompany-
ing Marge on a shopping trip, Spenser discovers the body of a
family friend and lawyer, Earl Maguire, who had planned to stop
by to set up the bar for the evening cocktail party. When Spenser
tells Marge that Maguire is dead on her living room floor, she replies,
"My God, the party's in six hours." She will let nothing—the disappearance of her son, a threat to her life (which she had received
the previous day), the murder of a close friend in her house—
interfere with the social life she has carefully arranged. No amount
of makeup or fancy clothes can mask for long the cruel selfishness
of the woman. Marge Bartlett is so consumed by self-love and a false
notion of what it means to be a contemporary woman that she has
become totally insensitive to those around her. Her attitude toward
her dog Punkin is sadly revealing: "But dogs are good. They don't
demand much of you; they just love you for what you are. Just accept you. I'm doing a sculpture of Punkin in clay. I want to capture
that trusting and undemanding quality." There is considerable hostility in Parker's attitude toward Marge and occasionally her portrait
degenerates into caricature. For example, Spenser describes her

going to make the ransom delivery dressed in an outrageously gaudy toreador outfit. And when he locates Kevin and asks her to accompany him to get her son, she declines, claiming her hair is mussed and she has nothing to wear. Such behavior only confirms the comic stereotype of the vain woman. But except for such obvious lapses, Parker succeeds in creating an all-too-convincing and sad character, one from whom Spenser admits he too would probably run if he lived in her house.

Susan Silverman theorizes that the explanation for Kevin's actions can be found in his family situation; she tells Spenser that the boy probably hasn't resolved his Oedipal conflicts and harbors hostility towards both parents. That hostility has driven him away from his family, and his confusion over gender identification, coupled with his unresolved sexual identity, has led him to Vic Harroway, a homosexual body builder who is leader of a group of runaway adolescents. Harroway, a former "Mr. Northeastern America," is a "body builder gone mad" who Spenser says "embodies every excess of body building that an adolescent fantasy could concoct." He may be Kevin's fantasy hero but he certainly isn't Spenser's, an avid weight lifter, or Parker's, who wrote a respected book on weight lifting for *Sports Illustrated*. Vic Harroway is the curse serious weight lifters have to bear, the body builder whose narcissistic efforts are aimed solely at appearance. However, to Kevin, desperately searching for an authority figure and for someone who will return his love, Harroway serves as the perfect model.

Kevin's hostility toward his parents at first takes the form of simply running away from them. But once he links up with Harroway, the hostility takes crueler form. First, a ransom note arrives, informing the Bartletts that Kevin has been kidnapped and will be killed unless a $50,000 ransom is paid. After the money is delivered, the police are directed to the spot where Kevin is said to be located. Instead they find a life-sized dummy which pops up out of an old hearse, a cruel prank. There is still no trace of Kevin. A phone call follows in which the speaker, a female, threatens to shoot Marge in her genitals, apparently because of her sexual promiscuity. It becomes increasingly clear that the kidnapping is a hoax, that Kevin did indeed leave home willingly, and that the threats and pranks are being done with his knowledge and approval as a way of getting back at his parents.

Spenser realizes that he has more than a simple missing-child case on his hands and knows that reuniting Kevin with his parents will not be easy. The solution to his problem, and the resolution of Kevin's Oedipal confusion, comes in a dramatic confrontation between Spenser and Harroway. Spenser brings the Bartletts to Harroway's apartment where Kevin is staying. Roger Bartlett tries to attack Harroway but is no match for his muscular opponent. Because Kevin has invested Harroway with almost superhuman stature, Spenser realizes that the only way he can break his spell over the boy is to demonstrate his vulnerability by defeating him in combat; he tells Kevin, "I'm going to beat your man, Kevin, so you'll know it can be done. Then I'm going to let you decide." Now cast into identical roles as substitute fathers, Spenser and Harroway engage in battle for control of Kevin.

What follows is a brutal hand-to-hand fight with the smaller but faster and more skillful Spenser beating the muscular Harroway. Kevin, stripped of the superman image he had of Harroway, is stunned. All he can do is stand immobile, his hands at his sides, weeping; his parents approach and he embraces them. Spenser has done his job; by defeating the substitute father he makes it possible for the boy to accept his parents again. His attitude toward his fallen opponent is interesting, however. As much as he dislikes him—for the suffering he has caused the Bartletts, for killing Earl Maguire (who died when Harroway struck him after he surprised him and Kevin when they returned to the Bartlett house to pick up some of Kevin's clothes), for insulting Susan, maybe even for giving weight lifting a bad name—he enjoys no Mike Hammer-like satisfaction in getting his revenge and pummelling his homosexual opponent. He tells Kevin: "He couldn't stop me. But there's no shame in that. It's just something I know how to do better than he does. He's a man, kid. I think he's a no-good sonova bitch. But he didn't quit. He went as far as he could, for you." Despite his animosity toward Harroway, Spenser recognizes that Harroway offered Kevin the one thing he needed and no one else offered—love.

Spenser's satisfaction over a job well done is short-lived, however, for a dark shadow soon clouds his success when he discovers the tragic implications of his involvement in the case. During his surveillance of Harroway, he witnessed an interesting incident: Harroway and Dr. Croft, the Bartlett's family doctor, surreptitiously exchanging a briefcase and an envelope in the Boston Common one evening. Later, after following Harroway to a local motel, he observes another suspicious scene: Fraser W. Robinson, another friend of the Bartletts, spending several hours in Harroway's room with a teenage girl. Spenser realizes that he has stumbled onto a drug and prostitution ring run by Harroway and Croft, with Croft supplying the drugs and the customers, Harroway the girls from his stable of runaways. For a price, Harroway would arrange anything—drugs, girls, or even the kind of offensive sexual orgy Robinson describes to Spenser involving five of Harroway's girls and a goat at the local legion hall.

Before his climatic battle with Harroway, Spenser had confronted Dr. Croft with his discovery and placed him in the custody of the Massachusetts State Police so he would be unable to warn Harroway that he was on his way. After settling matters with Harroway, Spenser attempts to recover Croft, but learns that the State Police have transferred him into the custody of Chief Trask of the Smithfield police. A phone call from his friend Lieutenant Quirk of the Boston police responding to his earlier inquiry into Croft's past alarms Spenser. He learns that his was the *second* inquiry about Croft; the first, according to police records, was made six years earlier by Chief Trask himself. Spenser rushes to the Smithfield police station only to discover his fears have been confirmed: Croft is dead, hanging from the bars of his cell. Spenser now knows the identity of Croft and Harroway's silent partner—Chief Trask who, having learned that Croft was wanted in Tacoma, Washington on a charge of performing an illegal abortion, blackmailed him into participating in his lucrative operation. Realizing that Croft was the only link between himself and Harroway, who was never told the identity of the third partner, Trask murdered him, making it appear that he had committed suicide. Spenser realizes that he has unwittingly delivered Croft to his death, and that he has no proof of Trask's involvement either in Croft's murder or in the prostitution ring. *The Godwulf Manuscript* ended with the promising sound of laughter, but *God Save the Child* ends on a more somber note, with Spenser wracked by anger, frustration, and guilt. He can think of nothing to do, so out of frustration he tosses Trask's gun through the window of the police station. He has succeeded in reuniting Kevin and his parents, but his dogged pursuit of Harroway has exposed a greater crime resulting in the death of Dr. Croft, a man who, while certainly not innocent of wrongdoing, was himself a victim of tragic circumstances. Croft's death reminds Spenser that he who walks the mean streets cannot always escape the effects of the corruption he seeks to root out; by accepting his own burden of guilt, Spenser recognizes that he is not immune to the hazards of the fallen world in which he operates.

The exposure of the prostitution ring and of Trask's involvement in it introduces a second theme in the novel—the pervasive corruption that lies just beneath the surface of affluent, respectable, middle-class society represented in the novel by the fictional town of Smithfield. To all appearances, Smithfield is a venerable community (the town meeting house dates back to 1681) whose most serious problem is an occasional runaway. But Spenser discovers otherwise: some of the most respected public figures in town are the most corrupt—Croft, a respected physician, is a member of the town's Board of Selectmen and the Conservation Commission, an advisor to the Board of Health, and a former planning Board member (the use of a doctor to represent the hypocritical relationship between respectability and crime is reminiscent of Chandler, who used corrupt doctors in at least four of his novels); Trask is the Chief of Police; Fraser Robinson and his fellow customers are prominent local citizens. Even before he learns about Trask's role in the prostitution ring, Spenser is cynical enough to suspect the worst, even in a town like Smithfield; he tells Susan, "Cops are public employees, like teachers and guidance counselors. They tend to give a community what it wants, not always what it should have. I mean if you happen to go for an evening out with five broads and a goat, and you are a man of some influence, maybe the cops won't prevent it." What he later realizes, of course, is that Trask not only does not prevent it, he actively promotes and profits by it. A new housing development being built in Smithfield by Roger Bartlett's construction company is called "Arden Estates." Smithfield is anything but the Forest of Arden as Shakespeare portrayed it, but the title of his play set in Arden, *As You Like It*, might certainly be used as a motto by those good citizens of Smithfield who know the right people and are rich enough to pay for sex any way they like it.

In *The Godwulf Manuscript* the crime was traced ultimately to the aberration of a sick mind. In *God Save the Child*, Parker is much more careful to locate the root of the problem in a familial and a social context, and then to draw an interrelationship between the two. For example, although Spenser initially believes he is working to solve a kidnapping case, and then discovers he has a murder to solve as well, the real crime in the novel is both simpler and more complex: the failure of the American family. (In fact, the investigation into Maguire's murder is of minor interest compared to Spenser's major concern, the reunion of Kevin and his family. Parker's *Three Weeks in Spring* is eloquent testimony to the importance he attaches to family.) In *God Save the Child*, Parker suggests a relationship between family failure and the more pervasive community corruption in Smithfield. Both are depicted as arising from similar causes— selfishness and abdication of responsibility. Whether it takes the form of Marge Bartlett's frantic pursuit of "creativity" or the sexually frustrated Smithfield citizens' pursuit of their jaded erotic fantasies, a narcissistic emphasis on self is the crucial factor. In both instances this factor is coupled with another, abdication of responsibility—the Bartletts are too preoccupied to fulfill their roles as parents, the Smithfield city fathers are too greedy to fulfill their duly constituted roles in the community.

Even before Trask's corruption is revealed, he is portrayed as an incompetent police officer. His handling of Kevin's apparent kidnapping discloses his lack of ability, and to listen to him is to realize he has watched too many police shows on television. He worries more about who will pay the per diem expenses for his men during a stakeout than he does about handling the stakeout properly. If he were the only policeman in the novel, the reader would be justified in concluding that Parker's attitude toward the police was negative. However, to counter the impression left by Trask, Parker includes the character of Lieutenant Healy of the Massachusetts State Police, chief investigator for the Essex County District Attorney's office. Healy is everything that Trask is not: intelligent, honest, effective, conscientious. Spenser makes a number of derogatory comments about police, criticizing them for their blind adherence to procedure, questioning their intelligence, even doubting their honesty. But he admires and respects Healy. Parker is not implying that all police are corrupt, just that public officials are as

vulnerable to corruption as anyone else. Being a police officer confers neither incompetence nor integrity automatically. The contrasting portraits of Trask and Healy illustrate the point.

A third important theme in *God Save the Child*, one the novel
shares with many of those of Chandler and Macdonald, is the decline of American civilization and the failure of the American Dream.
Like Marlowe and Archer, Spenser is often given to commenting on
the significance of what he sees around him. What he frequently
observes and records in ugly detail are the excesses of twentieth-
century, neon-and-plastic America, a picture he counters with a
heavily nostalgic view of the past, of a lost American purity and
innocence. Such a view is patently romantic, of course, but private
eyes have never successfully hidden their romanticism. After all,
most of them, at least since Marlowe, have been cast by their
creators in the anachronistic roles of knights displaced in the modern
city.

The opening sentence of the novel—"If you leaned way back
in the chair and cranked your neck hard over you could see the sky
from my office window, delft blue and cloudless and so bright it
looked solid."—sounds the note of loss that introduces this theme.
Spenser's office is in downtown Boston, so far removed from the
natural world that he must strain even to see the sky. The world
of the private eye is invariably an urban one, for Spenser that vast
megalopolis stretching from Boston to Virginia. This is what he sees
as he drives through the modern city:

> The expressway connects in Saugus to Route One and for the
> next ten miles is a plastic canyon of sub-sandwich shops, dis-
> count houses, gas stations, supermarkets, neocolonial furniture
> shops (vinyl siding and chintz curtains), fried chicken, big beef
> sandwiches, hot dogs cooked in beer, quarterpound hamburgers,
> pizzas, storm doors, Sears Roebuck, doughnut shops, stockade
> fencing—preassembled sections—restaurants that looked like log
> cabins, restaurants that looked like sailing ships, restaurants that
> looked like Moorish town houses, restaurants that looked like
> carwashes, carwashes, shopping centers, a fish market, a ski-
> mobile shop, an automotive accessory shop, liquor stores, a
> delicatessen in three clashing colors, a motel with an in-room
> steam bath, a motel with a relaxing vibrator bed, a car dealer,

an indoor skating rink attractively done in brick and corrugated plastic, a trailer park, another motel composed of individual cabins, an automobile dealership attractively done in glass and corrugated plastic, an enormous steak house with life-sized plastic cows grazing out front in the shadow of a six-story neon cactus, a seat cover store, a discount clothing warehouse, an Italian restaurant with a leaning tower attached to it.

Spenser concludes with the comment, "Maybe Squanto had made a mistake," a reference to the Indian who in 1621 aided the early Pilgrim settlers in Massachusetts. William Bradford, in *Of Plimouth Plantation*, describes Squanto as an instrument sent from God to teach the settlers how to grow corn and where to fish, and to guide them to "unknown places for their profit." Surely Squanto could have had no idea that the virgin forests and lush wilderness he showed the early Massachusetts settlers would degenerate to the urban ugliness that surrounds Spenser. This, sadly, is the story of America. With progress comes decline and loss. And ugliness.

All is not completely lost, however, for from time to time one still enjoys reminders of the past. On his drive north from Boston to Smithfield, Spenser notices Old Ironsides, the Bunker Hill Monument, and the Old North Church, and as he crosses the Mystic River Bridge he sees the outline of the coast in the bright sunlight. Suddenly he has a vision: "The brick and asphalt and neon were blurred by distance and sunshine and beneath it I got a sense of the land as it once must have been. The silent midsummer buzz of it and copper-colored near-naked men moving along a narrow trail." Such a vision is transitory, however, for the urban mess brings him back abruptly to the present. The contrast between his sense of the past and the reality of the present exposes the degeneration of the contemporary American landscape. The area he describes has become so overrun with expressways and elevated subway trains that if the British wanted to attack Bunker Hill today, Spenser notes wryly in *Mortal Stakes*, "they wouldn't be able to find it."

This bifocal view of America, a sort of then-and-now vision, places Spenser solidly in the company of his colleagues Philip Marlowe and Lew Archer, both of whom experienced similar visions. In *The Little Sister*, for example, Marlowe recalls the California he used to know:

I used to like this town. . . . A long time ago. There were trees along Wilshire Boulevard. Beverly Hills was a country town. Westwood was bare hills and lots offering at eleven hundred dollars and no takers. Hollywood was a bunch of frame houses on the interurban line. Los Angeles was just a big dry sunny place with ugly homes and no style, but goodhearted and peaceful. It had the climate they just yap about now. People used to sleep out on porches. Little groups who thought they were intellectual used to call it the Athens of America. It wasn't that, but it wasn't a neon-lighted slum either.

That Los Angeles exists now only in Marlowe's memory, having been superseded by a "big hard-boiled city with no more personality than a paper cup."

Or consider the view of Lew Archer, from the opening paragraph of *The Instant Enemy*:

There was light early morning traffic on Sepulveda. As I drove over the low pass, the sun came up glaring behind the blue crags on the far side of the valley. For a minute or two, before regular day set in, everything looked fresh and new and awesome as creation.

Or from the more recent *Sleeping Beauty*:

Traffic was still fairly light, and the day was clear enough to see the mountains rising in the east like the boundaries of an undiscovered country. I lapsed for a while into my freeway daydream: I was mobile and unencumbered, young enough to go where I had never been and clever enough to do new things when I got there.

The fantasy snapped in my face when I got to Santa Monica. It was just another part of the megalopolis which stretched from San Diego to Ventura, and I was a citizen of the endless city.

Archer realizes that the country has run out of frontiers, that there is no longer any territory to light out for. Like Archer, Spenser recognizes that Paradise (if it every really existed) has been irrevocably lost. He is enough of a realist to understand and to accept the nature of the world in which he lives, but he is also enough of a romantic to harbor nostalgic longings for a simpler, purer, less

defiled world. Innocence has given way to experience and this
has colored his view of everything, including crime. Spenser explains wistfully to Susan: "Used to be when you got a kidnapping
you assumed the motive to be greed and you could count on that
and work with it. You ran into a murder and you could figure lust
or profit as a starter. Now you gotta wonder if it's political, religious,
or merely idiosyncratic." This view, an amalgam of cynicism and
romanticism, characterizes to one degree or another all hard-boiled
detectives.

In *God Save the Child*, Parker blends plot, characterization,
style, and theme in a fresh and entertaining manner. Nothing is
wasted. The plot, for example, is handled much more effectively
than in *The Godwulf Manuscript*: it is fast-paced, suspenseful, without unnecessary complexity. Once Spenser and the reader realize
that the kidnapping is a hoax, the suspense shifts from whodunit to
the *why* of the incident. And although Spenser's uncovering of the
Smithfield sex ring, and of Trask's role in the operation, comes unexpectedly, its relationship to the initial crime is logically developed.
Parker manages this by having introduced all the principals—Trask,
Croft, Harroway, Fraser Robinson—early in the novel. Our surprise
comes only when we discover their secret relationships. Also, Parker
links the crimes thematically by showing that both arise from a
failure of responsibility.

An examination of three brief scenes in the novel illustrates
Parker's skill in sketching believable secondary characters, developing interesting scenes, and integrating the elements into the pattern
of the plot. In the first, Spenser visits Henry Cimoli, proprietor of
the Harbor Health Club, a much fancier version of Cimoli's Harbor
Gym where Spenser trained when he was a boxer. Cimoli confirms
Spenser's suspicion that Harroway is "queer as a square doughnut."
Spenser then pays a visit to the lavishly decorated studio of another
friend, gay fashion photographer Race Witherspoon. Miffed at being
considered a "gay data bank" by Spenser, he nevertheless gives him
the name of Harroway's usual hangout, a gay bar called The Odds'
End. Once there, Spenser feels extremely uncomfortable when he
discovers he is apparently very attractive to many of the customers.
Harroway finally arrives and Spenser is relieved when he leaves
and he can follow him. He traces him to the Boston Common, where
he observes the furtive meeting between Croft and Harroway and

the surreptitious exchange of items between them. Each of these scenes is vividly realized, each creates a distinct atmosphere and introduces different types of characters. Yet each is crucial in revealing a necessary item of information about Harroway's character and activities.

Nothing shows Parker's skill at integrating character, scene, and theme better than his description of the Bartlett's cocktail party. Spenser has been asked to keep an eye on Marge after she receives a death threat. Feeling as out of place as a "weed at a flower show," he nonetheless agrees to attend the party in case he is needed. The first jarring note comes when the reader realizes that the party is merrily going on in almost the exact spot where Earl Maguire was murdered only hours earlier, a fact which bothers Spenser but apparently no one else. Two other incidents produce the same uneasy feeling. During the party, Spenser receives a call from the Massachusetts State Police confirming that Maguire died of a broken neck. The party continues. Later he hears a recording of Billie Holiday singing her classic "God Bless the Child," a song about a deprived child which can be taken as an appropriate comment on Kevin Bartlett's predicament (and which gives the novel its title). No one but Spenser pays any attention to the song or its significance. The party continues.

This contrast between the frivolous and the tragic, and Marge's attempt to promote the former by ignoring the latter, parallels another contrast in the novel, that between respectability and corruption. The Bartlett's cocktail party is the gathering spot for many of Smithfield's finest citizens—doctors, businessmen, high school coaches, etc. We later learn how deeply involved many of these same people are in crime, either as operators or as customers. Parker's point is that these respectable citizens display as little concern for the existence of corruption in their midst as they do for Kevin's disappearance or Maguire's murder.

What unifies the separate themes of the novel—the family tragedy, the corruption within the community, the sense of lost values—is Parker's emphasis on relationships: the flawed—between Kevin and his parents; the failed—between Marge and Roger Bartlett; the unethical—between Croft and his patients; the corrupt—between Croft, Trask, and Harroway; the irresponsible—between Trask and the community of Smithfield. Set against this extensive catalogue of failures, however, are some positive and productive relationships: for example, the developing relationship between Susan and Spenser; or the professional relationship between Spenser and Lieutenant Healy; or the latent homosexual relationship between Kevin and Harroway which, despite its tragic effects, is at least based on love, a commodity in short supply in the novel.

God Save the Child shows that Parker is following the example of his predecessors, notably Chandler and Macdonald, in attempting to extend the dimensions of the detective novel. By combining the elements of the hard-boiled novel with his own interest in the psychology of his characters and their interrelationships, and with a critical attitude toward contemporary America and American values, Parker has written a mystery novel that resonates on several levels and suggests the direction in which his future Spenser novels will develop.

MORTAL STAKES

Midway in his career, Raymond Chandler admitted that "the time comes when you have to choose between pace and depth of focus, between action and character, menace and wit. I now choose the second in each case." On the evidence of *Mortal Stakes* (1975), his third Spenser novel, Parker appears to have made the same choices, emphasizing as Chandler did vivid characterization, serious exploration of theme, graceful and witty writing. The action begins on a sunny afternoon in Fenway Park. Spenser has been summoned by Harold Erskine, a Boston Red Sox official, who wants to hire him to find out if there is any evidence to verify his suspicion that Red Sox star pitcher Marty Rabb (next to Sandy Koufax, the best pitcher Spenser says he has ever seen) might be shading a game every now and then, perhaps even losing purposely on occasion. Spenser, a long-time baseball fan, agrees to take the case. His subsequent investigation proves that Erskine's suspicions are correct, but his personal feelings for Rabb and his wife present him with a dilemma, for he has learned that Rabb is being blackmailed by Red Sox broadcaster Bucky Maynard, who has discovered that Rabb's wife is a former prostitute who once appeared in a pornographic movie. To further complicate things, Maynard is blackmailing Rabb under orders from Frank Doerr, a gangster who has discovered an ingenious way to collect on Maynard's gambling debts to him: Maynard arranges for Rabb to lose a game every now and then, and Doerr makes a killing by betting on the games on the basis of his inside information. Spenser's tricky task is to save Rabb's professional career by getting Doerr off Maynard's back, and then Maynard off Rabb's back, without exposing Rabb. He succeeds, but only by becoming involved in a situation so distastefully violent that he questions his desire to continue his profession.

Although he is hired to investigate Rabb, Spenser soon realizes that Rabb's wife Linda is the key to the case. Suspicious about her story of how she met and married Rabb, Spenser manages to obtain her fingerprints and has his friend Lieutenant Healy send them to the F.B.I. He is informed that the prints belong to a Donna Burlington, who he learns was arrested in Redford, Illinois eight years earlier on a drug charge. Spenser heads for Redford, a small town on the Mississippi. There the local sheriff informs him that Donna Burlington was arrested at eighteen for possession of three marijuana cigarettes, given a suspended sentence, and placed on probation. Six weeks later, she fled with the local troublemaker, reportedly for New York, and has not been heard from since. Spenser visits the girl's parents, a poor worn-out couple who remind him of the pair in Grant Wood's famous painting, "American Gothic." The Burlingtons have accepted the disappearance of their restless daughter from their lives with the same tired resignation they accept everything. Spenser once again finds himself on the trail of a runaway, but with this twist: in *Mortal Stakes* the runaway has already been located; his task is to retrace the events of the past in order to discover how problem-teenager Donna Burlington became happily-married Linda Rabb, wife of one of baseball's most famous players.

Spenser follows Donna's trail to New York where, acting on a hunch, he checks the records of the Department of Social Services. He is right—Donna Burlington received welfare assistance shortly after arriving in New York. He locates her former landlady who remembers Donna and tells Spenser she believes Donna was a prostitute for a black pimp named Violet. Spenser has no trouble finding Violet at his usual place of business—leaning against a Cadillac Coupe de Ville in front of the Casa Grande bar:

> He was a black man probably six-three in his socks and about six-seven in the open-toed red platform shoes he was wearing. He was also wearing red and black argyle socks, black knickers and a chain mail vest. A black Three Musketeers' hat with an enormous red plume was tipped forward over his eyes. Subtle. All he lacked was a sign saying THE PIMP IS IN.

Many of Parker's characterizations begin this way, with a striking picture of the character's appearance. Violet is street wise, but so is Spenser, and their verbal exchanges are marked by rude wit, ethnic banter, sassy wisecracks, and jive talk. Violet's appearance in the novel is brief but memorable, and Spenser's success in gaining his confidence provides another lead—the name and address of Donna's next "employer," Mrs. Patricia Utley, the madam of a high-class call girl operation located in a fashionable townhouse on East Thirty-Seventh Street. The only thing the beautiful and sophisticated Mrs. Utley has in common with Violet is their profession. Spenser needs a different approach with her, so he tries a one-armed push-up. Charmed by his boyish assurance, Mrs. Utley agrees to have dinner with him and subsequently admits that Donna Burlington was indeed once in her employ. She also tells Spenser that Donna performed in one of her specialty films entitled "Suburban Fancy." Spenser discovers the missing link he has been searching for when he learns from Mrs. Utley that one of the names on the list of purchasers of the film is Lester Floyd, driver and constant companion of Red Sox broadcaster Bucky Maynard.

Spenser has solved the case. Donna Burlington, former prostitute, has become respectable Linda Rabb, wife of the star Red Sox pitcher who is being blackmailed by the team's broadcaster after he, by chance, happened to see the pornographic film she made. To protect his wife and young child, Rabb has been shading games every now and then according to Maynard's directions. Spenser's professional obligation is clear:

> I could report back to Erskine that it looked probable Rabb was
> in somebody's pocket and he could go to the D.A. and they
> could take it from there. I could get a print of the film and show
> Erskine and we could brace Rabb and talk about the integrity
> of the game and what he ought to do for the good of baseball
> and the kids of America. Then I could throw up.

He finds himself torn between his obligation to Erskine and the
Red Sox and his desire to help Marty and Linda Rabb. Erskine is
paying him for the information he has uncovered, but he feels a
deeper kinship with Rabb who, like himself, is torn between professional obligation and the appeal of something more personal.
Also, he likes Linda Rabb and feels that having overcome a number
of strikes against her—childhood poverty in Illinois, a drug conviction, prostitution in New York, performance in a stag film—she
has earned the right to a new life. As he explains to Mrs. Utley:
"She started out in life caught in a mudhole. And she's climbed out.
She has gotten out of the bog and onto solid ground and now she's
getting dragged back in."

Spenser is cynical about many things, but he remains stead-
fastly optimistic about an individual's ability to overcome the past.
One can never forget the past; Linda Rabb can't and is even willing
to admit to it publicly, an offer her husband refuses. But Spenser
feels she should not have to continue paying for her mistakes. His
attitude is founded on a conviction that is an essential component of
the traditional private eye's philosophy: even though one cannot
purify the world, cannot exorcise evil from it, one can attempt to
save deserving individuals. Nothing less, of course, can be expected
of the private eye when he assumes the role of knight, a role which
is predicated on the assumption that there are those who can be
(and ought to be) saved. Linda Rabb cannot change the past, and
her attempt to escape it by assuming a new identity has proved to
be ineffectual, with both Maynard and Spenser learning the truth.
So Spenser feels an obligation to help her and he commits himself to
her defense for a fee—two corn muffins and black coffee—which is
considerably less than the hundred dollars a day he charges Erskine.

Spenser's decision to help the Rabbs is made neither frivolously
nor quixotically; he understands all too well the difficulty he faces in
extricating them from their trap. Linda Rabb becomes furious with

him when he won't promise that he will at least be able to keep their names out of the mess. But Spenser, who in *The Godwulf Manuscript* invoked Frost's "Stopping by Woods on a Snowy Evening" in support of his belief in the inviolability of personal commitment, refuses to promise success in a venture whose outcome is doubtful. The private eye's word is often all he has, and Spenser's integrity prevents him from giving his word carelessly: "I care about promises and I don't want to make one I can't be sure I'll keep. It's important to me." Linda accuses him of being a "goddamned adolescent" and a game-playing child like her husband. Maybe she's right. But all games have rules and one of Spenser's primary rules involves his word. He will commit himself resolutely to the deed, i.e., rescuing the Rabbs, but not to the word, i.e., promising that everything will turn out all right in the end. He knows it may not turn out well at all.

Spenser learns from his bookie friend Lennie Seltzer that Bucky Maynard owes a large gambling debt to loanshark Frank Doerr. Doerr is the central figure in the scheme; he forces Maynard to pressure Rabb and then cleans up on bets based on his knowledge of how Rabb will pitch. Doerr is a tough character. Despite Spenser's attempts at levity (such as remarking that there is no "escape Doerr" to his problem), he knows the loanshark's reputation for viciousness. He decides to try the reasonable approach and cautiously asks him to lay off Rabb. Doerr will have none of Spenser's reasonableness: "I'm getting sick of you, Spenser. I'm sick of the way you look, and the way you dress, and the way you get your hair cut and the way you keep shoving your face into my work. I'm sick of you being alive and making wise remarks. You understand what I'm saying to you, turd?" When reason fails, Spenser tries muscle: he threatens to shoot Wally Hogg, Doerr's sidekick, and he crushes Doerr's hand in his desk drawer. This too fails to persuade Doerr to get off Rabb's back, but Spenser succeeds in angering him so much that he soon learns that Doerr is planning to kill him personally. Spenser's noble attempt to defend the Rabbs has instead resulted in his own death sentence.

The showdown between Spenser and Doerr is a scene right out of *High Noon*. (The comparison is not far-fetched, for commentators have long noted the kinship between the western hero and the private eye, who is a kind of urban cowboy. Spenser himself is aware of the parallel to *High Noon*, for when his stomach rumbles he wonders, "How come Gary Cooper's stomach never rolled," and the line, "Oh, to be torn 'tween love and duty," from the title song pops into his head.) The way Sheriff Will Kane (the Gary Cooper character) waits for the arrival of Frank Miller who has vowed to kill him, Spenser waits nervously for Frank Doerr at the Breakhart Reservation in Saugus, where he has arranged a meeting for six o'clock. He hides in the woods at 2:45 P.M. and watches the minutes tick by. The waiting becomes excruciating. At 4:15 P.M. Wally Hogg arrives and hides himself in the woods, planning to ambush Spenser. At 6:05 P.M. Doerr arrives and confronts Spenser, who has moved out of the woods but keeps a careful eye out for where he knows Hogg is hidden. Following an argument, Doerr reaches for his gut but is shot first by Spenser, who then wheels and fires at Hogg, killing him too. The bad guys are eliminated, peace is restored. In *High Noon*, Sheriff Kane, having lived up to the code that says a man must do what he must do, tosses his badge into the dust and leaves with his new wife on their honeymoon. Spenser, on the other hand, vomits.

If he were to apply Hemingway's famous test that what you feel good after doing is moral, what you feel bad after doing is immoral, then Spenser's sickness would verify his suspicions about the morality of his actions. Suffering pangs of conscience over killing two men he had set up, he visits the home of Susan Silverman, who makes her first appearance in the novel. The first thing he does is take a shower, but he stills feels as guilty as Lady Macbeth, whose famous words as she tries to wash the imagined blood from her hands, "Out, out, damned spot," he quotes as he leaves the shower. Susan understands Spenser's predicament, and tries to console him. She tells him "You are a good man. You are perhaps the best man I've ever known. If you killed two men, you did it because it had to be done. I know you. I believe it." Spenser doesn't need Susan's approval, but he does need (and gets) her understanding. She offers to make love with him, but he declines, satisfied instead with her support and understanding. Comforted, he falls asleep in her arms.

In each of his three novels thus far, Parker has provided a wide range of experiences for his hero, each designed to reveal a different facet of his character. Unlike Lew Archer, who solves most of his cases using the same techniques of persistent questioning and infinite understanding, Spenser must extend himself in different ways, risk himself in a variety of demanding situations. At the end of *God Save the Child*, for example, he was forced to admit his complicity in the murder of Dr. Croft, even though he acted with good intentions. Now he finds he has to deal with an even greater burden of guilt after he kills two men. What bothers him so much is not the killing of the two (he had killed two men in *The Godwulf Manuscript*), but the way he did it, arranging an ambush for them. Justifying his actions as self-defense does not entirely erase the guilt. In *Mortal Stakes*, Parker shows Spenser's compassion through his defense of the Rabbs, but he also reveals Spenser's vulnerability, a quality that proclaims not his weakness but his humanness.

In addition to Susan, Brenda Loring, whose laughter cheered Spenser up at the end of *The Godwulf Manuscript*, also makes a return appearance in *Mortal Stakes*. Spenser is sexually involved with both women, but each offers him something more important than bedtime companionship. First of all, his conversations with the women allow him to analyze character motivation or consider alternative directions for his investigations. More importantly, each woman fills a particular need for Spenser: Brenda, the more fun-loving of the two, is a perfect companion for an afternoon at the ballpark or a picnic in the Public Garden; Susan provides something more valuable. When he finds himself in difficulty, Spenser turns to her: "I wanted to talk about things I had trouble talking about. Susan Silverman was good at that, Brenda was for fun and wise-cracks and she did a terrific picnic, but she wasn't that much better than I was a talking about hard things." (In subsequent novels, Brenda drops out and Susan, combining both roles, comes to play an increasingly important function as a modifying and humanizing influence on Spenser.)

Brenda and Susan are two members of a repertory company of characters who reappear in each of Parker's novels. Frank Belson and Martin Quirk, policemen from *The Godwulf Manuscript*, return to assist Spenser in his investigation in *Mortal Stakes*. Lieutenant Healy, with whom he worked in *God Save the Child*, recommends Spenser to Red Sox official Harold Erskine. Henry Cimoli, proprietor of the Harbor Health Club, also makes a return apperance. By allowing Spenser to maintain a number of personal and professional relationships from one novel to the next, Parker avoids the gloomy air of loneliness that often haunts the Chandler and Macdonald novels and gives his hero an anchor of stability and continuity in a world of loneliness and disorder.

As noted earlier, Parker is a sports enthusiast, and Spenser reflects his interest in such activities as jogging, boxing, weight lifting, and baseball. And so a novel about baseball from a writer with Parker's interests is not at all surprising. However, his choice of a baseball player as a central character in *Mortal Stakes* demands closer examination, for the game of baseball itself becomes an important symbol in the novel. Baseball is a game of pattern and balance, its carefully delineated rules imposing a sense of order on disorder. In *God Save the Child*, Spenser defined its quality this way: "Order and pattern, discernable goals strenuously sought within rigidly defined rules. A lot of pressure and a lot of grace, but no tragedy." If baseball is viewed as a symbol of order, then any threat to that order, say by shading points in a game, is not only a serious offense to the integrity of the national pastime, it is also a reminder that nothing is inviolate, safe from the intrusion of disorder. On one level, Spenser's investigation of Marty Rabb is simply an attempt to determine if a player is violating the rules of the game, but on another, it can also be seen as his attempt to preserve his image of baseball as an enduring symbol of order in a disorderly world. (Parker, of course, is not alone in detecting the symbolic possibilities inherent in baseball; such writers as Bernard Malamud, Philip Roth, and Robert Coover have all written novels that use baseball in a symbolic manner.)

Parker also employs another symbol of order and disorder in the novel. To kill time one afternoon Spenser visits the aquarium and is fascinated by the beautiful order of all the fish in the tank. He watches them gliding "in silent pattern around and around the tank, swimming a different strata, sharks and groupers and turtles and fish I didn't know in the clear water. They were oblivious of me and seemed oblivious of each other as they swam in a kind of implacable order around and around the tank." The fish have developed a pattern of order to forestall what would otherwise be chaos and disorder. As he turns away from the fish, Spenser notices the penguins only six feet away, with no separation of a glass wall between him and the animals: "The smell of fish and, I supposed, penguin, was rank and uninsulated. I didn't like it. The silent fish in the lucid water were fantasy. The smelly penguins were real." The fish in the protected tank and the smelly penguins outside it become an interesting metaphor for the opposing forces of order and disorder depicted in the novel. Together with the symbol of baseball, the aquarium scene suggests a metaphysical view of the world that is typical of much hard-boiled detective fiction.

A bit of crime fiction history is in order here. The hard-boiled novel appeared in America in the 1920s as a reaction to the prevailing form of detective fiction popular at the time, the ratiocinative novel perhaps best illustrated by the Sherlock Holmes stories. The ratiocinative novel operates on a shared assumption between reader and writer that there is a normal order to things that is temporarily disrupted by a crime. In this type of novel, the detective applies reason and logic to the problem, solves the crime, banishes disorder, and restores things to their usual ordered condition. In the period following World War I, many readers and writers began to view the world differently: for them, crime could no longer be viewed simply as an aberration from the normal scheme of things, it was an integral part of it. This view of the randomness and disorder of the world received its fullest expression in the writings of such existentialists as Kafka; and in the years that followed in Sartre and Camus. Detective fiction was not immune to this metaphysical perception. Rejecting the comfortable, secure world portrayed in ratiocinative fiction, writers like Dashiell Hammett and several of his contemporaries in *Black Mask* magazine developed a new type of crime fiction reflecting their view that although crimes may be solved, disorder can never be banished. Thus the hard-boiled novel came on the scene, and later writers like Chandler and Macdonald, while developing according to their own interests and talents, nevertheless adhered to that same perception. The world portrayed in *Mortal Stakes* is metaphysically consistent with this tradition.

The aquarium scene functions much like the famous story Sam Spade tells Brigid O'Shaughnessy in *The Maltese Falcon* about a man named Flitcraft, who narrowly escapes death one day when a falling beam barely misses hitting him. He is so shaken by his experience of the tenuousness of existence that he abandons his family, moves away, and starts a new life based upon his sudden and dra-

matic awareness of the irrationality and purposelessness of life.
Eventually, however, after the shock of his experience has worn
off, he makes his adjustments and Spade finds him living a life that
is a carbon copy of the one he left behind. Not everyone can remain
true to his perceptions, no matter how dramatic they might be.
(Flitcraft plays no active role in the novel. However, the story of
his experience is a metaphysical parable that helps to explain
Spade's view of the world.) In similar fashion, Parker employs
Spenser's visit to the aquarium as something more than a way for
him to kill time; it establishes a context for understanding his perception of the world and underscores his need to devise a personal
and professional code which takes into account the reality of both
order and disorder.

Spenser defines his code during a conversation with Marty
Rabb. He suggests to Rabb that the easiest way out of his difficulty
would be for his wife to make a public confession about her past,
thus making blackmail impossible. Rabb, the all-American jock,
refuses, arguing that it is his duty to protect his family's honor.
Spenser replies, "Grow up, Marty . . . The world's not all that clean.
You do what you can, not what you oughta. You're involved in
stuff that gets people dead. If you can get out of it with some
snickers in the bullpen and some embarrassment for your wife, you
call that good. You don't call it perfect. Maybe you don't even call
it happy. But you call it better than it was." Spenser, speaking with
the authority of experience, tries to reason with Rabb, whose attitude strikes Spenser as dangerously naive.

Spenser's literary allusions are usually significant, and a phrase
he uses to describe Rabb is especially revealing. On his first visit
to Rabb's apartment, Spenser describes him waiting at the door:
"There was something surrealistic about the way his head appeared
to violate the fearful symmetry of the hall." Only someone familiar
with William Blake's poem, "The Tiger," would use the phrase
"fearful symmetry," which Blake used to describe the awe-inspiring
beauty and danger of the powerful tiger. And anyone familiar with
"The Tiger" is likely to know Blake's companion poem, "The Lamb,"
written several years earlier. "The Lamb" appeared in a volume of
Blake's poems called *Songs of Innocence* and describes a childlike
view of the world, a perception of reality as safe, secure, comfortable. Blake answers the question, "Little Lamb, who made thee?"

unhesitatingly—God made the lamb. However, five years later he published another book of poems called *Songs of Experience* (one of which is "The Tiger"), that reflects a darker, more skeptical view. The answer to the question about the creator of the lamb was easy; the question he raises in the later poem is more difficult. If God created the beautiful and harmless lamb, could he have also created the equally beautiful but far more dangerous and threatening tiger? The simplicity of Blake's earlier view has given way to a more complex one which takes into account an awareness of the reality of evil. Experience has taught Blake that the world is populated by *both* lambs and tigers, and to ignore the "fearful symmetry" of the tiger is to remain innocent about the way things really are. (During Spenser's visit to Susan's home after he shoots Doerr and Hogg, he utters some lines, "There is a knife blade in the grass . . . And a tiger lies just outside the fire," which echo Blake's tiger reference in a restatement of the view that disorder constantly threatens to intrude upon order.)

Rabb cannot deal with his problem effectively because he evaluates his situation from a naive point of view: he alone will protect his wife and child, everything will turn out fine. His wife's accusation that he is still a child playing games is all too true. Spenser has experienced too much, seen too much of the world's evil, smelled its fishy smell too often, to accept Rabb's naive solution to his dilemma. If Rabb won't help himself, then he must do what he can to help.

But Spenser is himself stung by Linda Rabb's charge that, with all his talk about codes and promises, he too is playing adolescent games. Spenser fears that she might be right, that he might be playing with other people's lives in order to justify his code of behavior. Afflicted with self-doubt, he returns to his office and does what any self-respecting private eye would do—he reaches for his trusty bottle of bourbon. As he begins to get drunk and starts grinning at his file cabinet, his mind wanders tipsily and he starts to wax poetic. Some lines from Robert Frost's "Two Tramps in Mud Time" occur to him. The poem describes a scene in which the narrator is interrupted by the appearance of two lumberjacks while he is busy chopping wood. He senses that they are looking at him accusingly as one who has no right to play at what for them is a livelihood, i.e., splitting wood. He is doing for love what they must do out of necessity, as their job. The narrator confesses that his object in life is to "unite my avocation and my vocation," and the poem concludes with these lines, which Parker quotes as the epigraph to his novel and from which he derives its title:

> Only where love and need are one,
> And the work is play for mortal stakes,
> Is the deed ever really done
> For Heaven and the future's sakes.

Frost's words could serve as a motto for any number of private eyes whose heroic dedication to their profession arises from their ability to combine avocation and vocation. Spenser, like the Continental Op, Sam Spade, Philip Marlowe, Lew Archer, and countless others before him, does what he does *because he wants to*. All of them are like Frost's woodcutter, performing a task because they enjoy it, and all of them at times endure the same scorn from the police that Frost's speaker faces from the lumberjacks, who feel that chopping wood should be left to the professionals, not to amateurs. But the advantage the private eye has is the same one that Frost's speaker has—a special dedication, commitment, and personal satisfaction in performing the task. And maybe also a bit of pride at showing the professionals that he is better at their own job than they are.

    Not that the private eye is immune from nagging doubts about his chosen vocation; most question themselves more scrupulously than others do. Why not get out of the field, settle down, get a steady job? If you are so interested in justice, why not become a policeman? Spenser jokes that if he returned to the police department, he wouldn't "need to worry about charger feed and armor polish," a wry reference to the lonely and not very lucrative role of knight the private eye often plays. But becoming a cop again wouldn't satisfy Spenser's passion for justice, concern for the innocent and defenseless, and interest in the truth. Like his fellow private eyes, he endures suffering, loneliness, and periods of self-doubt because he does what satisfies him.

    Equally persuasive as an argument against returning to the police department is his realization that he would have to surrender much of his freedom. He left the police originally because of "insubordination," an unwillingness to follow department rules. As a private investigator, he is free to follow his instincts and to set his own rules. But if one is this free, where are the constraints? If one follows Spenser's advice to Rabb that you do what you can, not what you ought to, then what limits are there? This is one of the ethical questions raised in *Mortal Stakes*, and the moral ambiguity of the whole issue gives the novel a seriousness of purpose that the first two Spenser novels, for all their virtues, lacked.

What is it that differentiates a Lew Archer or a Philip Marlowe from a Mike Hammer? Each emerged from the same hard-boiled tradition, each pursues justice (as he defines it) on his own. But no one would mistake Lew Archer for Mike Hammer. The essential difference between them is the limits to their freedom. Since the private eye works alone, he has few external restraints to his freedom. He must therefore define his own limits, establish a code that will allow him to function effectively but in accord with his ethical values. This is what concerns Spenser in *Mortal Stakes*. On at least two occasions, he makes judgments that call his ethics into question. The first is handled rather easily. He has been hired by Harold Erskine to gather information about Marty Rabb and report back to him. When the information proves damaging to Rabb, he withholds it and decides instead to work to save Rabb. When he finally does report to Erskine, he lies to him, assuring him that there is no truth to his suspicions about Rabb. His decision is understandable. The extenuating circumstance of Rabb's succumbing to intense pressure being exerted by blackmailers and Spenser's commitment to protect Rabb's family outweigh the breaking of a few baseball rules, especially when the only one to profit by Rabb's cheating is Frank Doerr. Spenser, the reader would agree, makes the right decision, one he clearly would not have been free to make if he were investigating for the police. The second matter—his killing of Frank Doerr and Wally Hogg—is more ambiguous. He can justify his actions as self-defense, but the nagging fact remains that he set up both men for the ambush. This concerns him deeply enough to force a reexamination of his whole code of behavior.

In the final chapter of the novel, Spenser reviews with Susan the moral implications of his actions. Structurally, the scene is out of place, anticlimatic and unnecessary to the action which has been completed. Nevertheless it reminds us that a private eye like Spenser

is a kind of existential hero who must create and constantly reexamine his code of behavior, which is based on such things as an
awareness of his freedom, a realization of the need for self-imposed
limits to that freedom, and an understanding of the nature of the
world in which he exists. Spenser is particularly bothered by the
realization that his and Rabb's code did not work. He explains to
Susan:

> See, being a person is a kind of random and arbitrary business.
> You may have noticed that. And you need to believe in some-
> thing to keep it from being too random and arbitrary to handle.
> Some people take religion, or success, or patriotism, or family,
> but for a lot of guys those things don't work. A guy like me. I
> don't have religion or family, that sort of thing. So you accept
> some system of order and you stick to it. For Rabb it's playing
> ball. You give it all you got and you play hurt and don't com-
> plain and so on and if you're good you win so the more you
> win the more you prove you're good. But for Rabb it's also
> taking care of the wife and kid and the two systems came into
> conflict. He couldn't be true to both. And now he's compromised
> and he'll never have the same sense of self he had before.

Because he knows his code didn't work either, Spenser also worries
about his own sense of self. Susan argues that he ought to outgrow
all this "Hemingwayesque nonsense," but to Spenser what Hemingway said about the necessity for devising a code of behavior is
anything but nonsense. The pervasive influence of Hemingway can
be seen in all of Parker's writing; one can detect it in *Mortal Stakes*
in the conception of Spenser's character and in the picture of the
world that the novel presents. All the talk about the need for rules,
for imposing order on disorder, reminds us of Hemingway's story,
"A Clean, Well-Lighted Place," which describes the conflict between
order and disorder, and which uses the clean, well-lighted cafe as a
metaphor for the structure man devises to impose order on the
nada, the nothingness of the universe which is always threatening
to invade. In addition, the manner in which Hemingway's characters—from Nick Adams to Frederic Henry to Santiago the fish-
erman—confront their challenges with a code of behavior which is
nothing more than a series of promises made to themselves has
obviously influenced Parker's conception of his hero. Spenser's ac-

tions in *Mortal Stakes* demonstrate that he shares Hemingway's perception that we live in a world characterized by disorder and uncertainty, but that it can be faced honorably and confidently with a coded pattern of behavior. (It is interesting to note that Joan Parker's sudden discovery of her cancer, recounted in *Three Weeks in Spring*, occurred during the writing of *Mortal Stakes* and may well have intensified this concept of the uncertainty and arbitrariness of life that infuses the novel.) But the novel also demonstrates that such a code of behavior is imperfect and does not apply equally to all situations. Marty Rabb found that his code—the code of the athlete that says one gives 110% to the game—had to be violated for a better reason, his family. Spenser knows that his code—that you never kill people except involuntarily—was violated when he arranged an ambush for two men, even though his action was motivated by his desire to save Rabb and his family and, not incidentally, to save himself from a man who had vowed to kill him.

High Noon comes to mind again here, but less for the parallel between Sheriff Kane and Spenser than for that between Kane's new bride Amy and Spenser. Amy is a Quaker committed to nonviolence. When her husband decides he must stay in Hadleyville and fight Frank Miller and his gang, she decides she must leave him, even though they have been married for less than an hour. However, when the Miller gang later moves and surrounds her husband, who is facing them all alone, she picks up a gun and shoots one of the men as he is about to shoot her husband. She has violated her Quaker code, and will have to live with that realization, but she also saved her husband's life. Sometimes the code won't work. Spenser comes to understand that the code is only a guide, a way of managing a slippery universe, not a panacea for its problems. Spenser gets a whiff of his own mortality as a result of his actions, but that is the price you must pay when you play the game for mortal stakes. Perhaps the price you pay for being human.

In his dissertation, Parker quotes a passage from Robert Warshow's essay on the Western movie, which might serve as an appropriate comment on *Mortal Stakes*:

> . . . the Westerner comes into the field of art only when his moral code, without ceasing to be compelling, is also seen to be imperfect. The Westerner at his best exhibits a moral ambiguity

which darkens his image and saves him from absurdity; this
ambiguity arises from the fact that, whatever his justifications,
he is a killer of men.

Mortal Stakes is Parker's best novel precisely because it recognizes
the ambiguity Warshow describes. It is Parker's most assured in its
handling of material, it has interesting and believable characters
and a strong sense of atmosphere. But above all it raises important
questions about the role of the private eye, and it dramatizes such
moral issues as the authenticity of personal behavior and the struggle to maintain ethical sensitivity in an imperfect and violent world.
And it does all this without sacrificing the pace, suspense, and action
of a good detective novel. In seeking to do his best as a private eye,
Spenser learns something about himself; in the process he grows
from a believable and likable private eye into a convincing and
vulnerable human being.

PROMISED LAND

Although each of Parker's first three Spenser novels was critically
well received, it was his fourth, *Promised Land* (1976), that brought
him widespread recognition—it received an Edgar Award as the
best mystery novel of 1976. Nevertheless, despite the acclaim it
must be admitted that the novel is something of a disappointment,
and its failures are in areas that, ironically, were responsible for the
success of the first three novels. Parker's strength has never been in
his plotting, and the shaky plot of *Promised Land* confirms this. His
strongest features are characterization and dialogue, yet there is an
overemphasis on character analysis and an excessive talkiness that
upsets the novelistic balance in *Promised Land* and results in an
often lifeless work that lacks the sparkle and vitality of the first
three Spenser books.

The case begins as another search for a runaway. Spenser is

hired by Harv Shepard to find his wife Pam, an apparently happily married wife and mother of three who has left their family home in Hyannis, Massachusetts. Spenser has a good track record when it comes to finding runaways, and it doesn't take him long to locate Pam living with two radical feminists in New Bedford, Massachusetts. But after talking with her, he decides to delay telling her husband where she is until he can do a little marriage counseling before their reunion. However, before they can be reunited, the plot takes several turns for the worse. First, Pam accompanies her radical friends on a bank robbery during which a guard is shot and killed by one of the women. Pam now finds herself wanted by the police on armed robbery and murder charges. Then Spenser discovers that Harv has been dipping into his company's escrow account and has been forced to borrow $30,000 from King Powers, a loanshark who is threatening him because he cannot repay the money. Now instead of a simple missing wife case, Spenser is faced with the more serious problem of rescuing Pam from the police and Harv from the mob before he can reunite them, and he must do it on his own, since he has been fired by Harv for asking too many probing questions about his business affairs. He solves his dilemma by devising an elaborate scheme in which he arranges to have Pam's radical friends buy a carload of guns from King Powers with the proceeds of their bank robbery. Then he tips off the police and strikes a deal whereby they will spring a trap to catch the bank robbers and the slippery King Powers. In return, the police agree to let the Shepards go free.

The plot complications and their resolution are not entirely credible. Parker's first novel, *The Godwulf Manuscript*, exhibited plot weaknesses that he managed to avoid in his next two novels: in *God Save the Child*, for example, the complications involving the murder of Dr. Croft and the exposure of Trask's corruption were believable, developed organically from the previous action, and were consistent with the theme of corruption in the novel; in *Mortal Stakes*, since the plot complications were essentially completed before the action of the novel began, the plot unfolded as Spenser pieced together the events from Linda Rabb's past. And the resolution of the plot was handled skillfully; Spenser reviewed his options, tried unsuccessfully to reason with Frank Doerr, and only when that failed did he decide on a more violent course of action which resolves the situation convincingly. But there are several weaknesses in the plot of *Promised Land*. First of all, inadequate motivation is given to explain why an essentially good woman like Pam Shepard would become involved in a bank robbery. The same question was asked about Patty Hearst, but in her case one had to consider the effects of her kidnapping and possible brainwashing by her captors. There are no comparable circumstances to explain Pam's behavior. Second, Harv's involvement with gangster King Powers is a fairly gratuitous element in the plot. There are a number of other ways to show a man becoming financially overextended. The introduction of mob involvement in the novel exists primarily to give Spenser a convenient way of getting Pam off the hook by providing the bait to catch her accomplices. Finally, the resolution of the plot places Spenser in a role that is inconsistent with the character we have seen in the previous books. In *Mortal Stakes*, for example, he became involved, but only reluctantly, in a situation which led to his killing two men, actions which disturbed him because they called into question his ethical code, but which he performed because of his personal commitment to the Rabbs. In *Promised Land*, he not only unhesitatingly arranges an ambush that is clearly illegal, but he does so for a couple he admits he doesn't even like. The demands of the plot require him to modify his ethical principles rather cavalierly for two people, one a bank robber, the other an embezzler.

It should be noted that although Spenser often assumes the knightly role played by many private eyes before him, he seldom defends the purely innocent. In *The Godwulf Manuscript*, for example, although Terry Orchard is innocent of the murder she is charged with, she was in fact involved with the radical group that stole the priceless manuscript. In *God Save the Child*, Kevin Bartlett willingly participated in the scheme to extort $50,000 from his parents. In *Mortal Stakes*, Linda Rabb was a prostitute and performer in stag movies, and her husband did occasionally cheat when he pitched. Yet in each case there are mitigating circumstances: either the person is innocent of the particular crime in question, like Terry Orchard, or is forced to become involved in criminal activity, either by emotional needs, like Kevin Bartlett, or by pressure from blackmailers, like Marty Rabb. Spenser's defense of the less-than-entirely-innocent is consistent with Parker's view, dramatized in *Mortal Stakes*, that this is an imperfect world and the people who live in it cannot be expected to be perfect. It takes nothing away from Spenser's noble role as knight to admit that those he helps are frequently flawed individuals.

Consequently, there is nothing essentially surprising about Spenser's involvement with the Shepards in *Promised Land*. What is surprising is that Spenser agrees to defend, without apparent qualm, a woman who was stupid enough to get involved in a bank robbery during which one of her accomplices shot and killed an elderly bank guard. There is no doubt about her guilt, and Spenser makes no excuses for what he calls her "vicious and mindless god-damn crime." His efforts are not directed at establishing her innocence, only at getting her off the hook. And her husband needs to be rescued from the clutches of King Powers because he borrowed money to cover his dipping into the escrow funds of his land development company. If he had avoided the temptation to embezzle the funds in the first place, there would be no need to rescue him from a character like Powers. Spenser cannot justify his defense of the Shepards on the grounds of personal commitment; his opinion of them is clear: "Saps. I was disgusted with both of them. It's an occupational hazard, I thought. Everyone gets contemptuous after a while of his clients. Teachers get scornful of students, doctors of patients, bartenders of drinkers, salesmen of buyers, clerks of customers. But, Jesus, they were saps." Instead of acting like a defender of truth and justice, Spenser in *Promised Land* appears to be little more than a hired professional valued for his ability to perform a dirty job for people who are unable to save themselves from their own stupidity. His activities when he isn't working actively to save the Shepards—dining, dancing, and romancing with Susan like a salesman combining business and a Cape Cod vacation with his wife—only reinforce this perception.

With the motive of personal commitment considerably diminished, Parker suggests two others to justify Spenser's efforts on behalf of the Shepards. First, there is the simple challenge of the situation. Susan repeats the accusation made by Linda Rabb in *Mortal Stakes* that Spenser hasn't outgrown adolescent gameplaying; of his work, she says, "There is an element of play in it for you, a concern for means more than ends." Devising an elaborate plan that will work is the challenge, and it appears to interest Spenser more than the legal (to say nothing of the moral) implications of his actions, something that could not be said of him in the previous novels. In *Mortal Stakes*, for example, Spenser expressed grave doubts about the morality of arranging an ambush in which two men were killed, even though he finally justified it on the grounds of self-defense. But he gives little thought to the ethical questions of illegal entrapment, double-crossing, withholding evidence, and obstruction of justice arising from his action in *Promised Land*. Perhaps he feels such justification unnecessary because he is delivering wanted criminals to the police, including some radical feminists who intend to obtain guns illegally anyway. But there remains a nagging question about his motivation, for he is neither defending his own life, as he did in *Mortal Stakes*, nor protecting the innocent. And since he has been fired by Harv he is no longer even working for pay. The whole thing smacks a little of professional showing off, of demonstrating his ingenuity by flim-flamming the tough King Powers. (Spenser even jokingly suggests that there be a little Scott Joplin music in the background, a reference to the ragtime music which provided the lively accompaniment for the movie *The Sting*. Making light of a messy situation does little to ameliorate it.) Finally, the challenge is largely intellectual, for he risks little in the setup, since police from several agencies are handling the whole situation and their presence in such large numbers all but guarantees success.

More convincing as an explanation for Spenser's involvement than the challenge of the situation, however, is his attitude toward the Shepards' marital dilemma. To all appearances, Pam is a happy wife and mother, a typical American housewife. But one day, after twenty-two years of marriage, she ups and walks away, leaving her family for no apparent reason. Spenser's first thought is that Pam has joined the growing army of American housewives who "read two issues of *Ms.* magazine, see Marlo Thomas on a talk show and decide they can't go on. So they take off." But as he learns more about her (and with the helpful prodding of Susan Silverman), he becomes more sympathetic to her problem. He learns, for example, that lately she has been picking up young jocks and muscle men in local bars. When Pam later confesses that she has been unable to have sex with her husband for two years, Spenser realizes that her sexual promiscuity was an attempt to resolve her own insecurity and discover her sexual identity. She admits to feeling overwhelmed and smothered by Harv's constant affection which, she said, deprived her of her own space. So she runs away in search of herself, her identity, her sexuality. (Her action reminds us of Kevin Bartlett who ran away from home in *God Save the Child* for much the same reasons, except he was looking for love and she was running away from it.) Spenser decides that instead of telling her husband where she is, he will try to arrange a reconciliation. Unfortunately, his delay in returning Pam to her husband results in her involvement in the bank robbery and murder. It never occurs to Spenser that without his meddling, Pam's problems might be far less serious.

Spenser exchanges his knightly role as defender of the innocent for a new one, marriage counselor. His view of his function has altered significantly from *The Godwulf Manuscript*, where he pointedly refused to accompany Terry Orchard to the reunion with her parents because it was "family business." In *Promised Land*, Spenser has no such qualms about involving himself in "family business." During a conversation with Chief Slade of the Barnstable police, Spenser admits that he left the police because he wanted to do more than they do. Slade remarks, disgustedly, "Social work." Like Lew Archer, Spenser finds himself worrying more and more about the happiness of his clients, with the result that robbery and murder appear to be of secondary importance when compared with Pam's unhappiness. Instead of surrendering Pam to the police, he hides her in his apartment and plots for her return to her husband because, as he explains to her, "You've got kids that need a mother, you've got a husband that needs a wife. You've got a life and it needs you to live it. You're a handsome intelligent broad in the middle of something that could still be a good life." The demands of justice take a back seat to the claim of personal happiness, which Spenser equates with the reconciliation of the Shepards and the resumption of their married life.

There is another parallel between Spenser and Lew Archer, one more complex than a simple concern for the happiness of others. Archer often finds himself in situations, usually involving a lost son or father, which reflect his and, more importantly, his creator's obsession. If Parker can be said to have any obsession, it is his family. *Three Weeks in Spring* testifies to the love and affection that exist between Parker and his wife—he has admitted that the fundamental relationship in his life is that with his wife. So when

Spenser defends the family and devotes his energies to saving the
Shepards' marriage, or the Rabbs' in *Mortal Stakes*, or reuniting
the Orchards in *The Godwulf Manuscript* or the Bartletts in *God
Save the Child*, he is reflecting Parker's obsession. Spenser's comment to Pam, "I am sick of people, whatever sex, who dump the
kids and run off: to work, to booze, to sex, to success. It's irresponsible" expresses his opinion rather explicitly. Pam wonders whether
Spenser might not possibly be more interested in defending the
concept of marriage rather than in insuring her personal happiness.
She asks, "Why do you want Harvey and me back together? I'm
not sure that's your business. Or is it just America and apple pie.
Marriages are made in heaven, they should never break up?"
Spenser says he doesn't "give a goddamn about the sanctity of
marriage," but his efforts on the Shepards' behalf suggest that he
has seen enough unhappiness, in children as well as in husbands
and wives, to devote himself to preserving at least one marriage he
judges worth saving.

Spenser's defense of the Shepards' marriage, however, complicates his own relationship with Susan. For despite his goal of
restoring their shaky marriage, he rejects the idea of marriage with
Susan. Pam's crisis affects Susan deeply and prompts her to reexamine her relationship with Spenser. While admitting that it is
satisfying in every way—emotional, physical, intellectual—she concludes that it lacks one crucial element: she tells him, "It is mo-
mentary and therefore finally pointless. It has no larger commitment,
it involves no risk, and therefore no real relationship." Susan's
complaint is reminiscent of W. H. Auden's comment about marriage: "Like everything which is not the involuntary result of fleeting
emotion but the creation of time and will, any marriage, happy or
unhappy, is infinitely more interesting and significant than any
romance, however passionate." Spenser appears to endorse Auden's
view when it comes to the Shepards, but not when it involves his
own situation. He can affirm his love for Susan through his actions
and gestures, but he refuses the symbolic affirmation of their relationship that marriage involves. Spenser is trapped in a dilemma
of his own making. If it is so important to save the Shepards' marriage, then why won't he marry Susan whom he obviously loves.
(One measure of his commitment to her is his refusal to succumb
to the temptation of making love with Pam while she is staying in

his apartment; he is proud of his hard-fought victory of virtue over tumescence.) Restoration of the Shepards' marriage, however unhappy at present, is Spenser's stated goal, but in pursuing it he unwittingly exposes his own hypocrisy. By his actions he seems to be saying, "married life is important for you (because *I* say so), but not for me (because *I* say so)." His attitude so angers Susan that she walks out on him.

One of Spenser's more attractive features has always been his educability. Parker here follows the example of Raymond Chandler who, notably in *The Long Goodbye*, showed how the detective novel could be used to portray the education of its hero. *God Save the Child* dramatized Spenser's acceptance of his share of guilt for the tragic results of actions which he set into motion. The events in *Mortal Stakes* reminded him about the uncertain nature of the world and taught him the difficulty of maintaining a code of behavior in all situations. In *Promised Land*, his involvement in the Shepard case forces him to reconsider his own attitude toward marriage, to examine it in personal rather than abstract terms, and to assess his relationship with Susan in light of his attitudes toward the Shepards. Spenser is not inflexible, and he slowly comes to realize the inconsistencies of his views and to recognize the necessity of making the commitment Susan demands. At the end of the novel he proposes marriage.

The logical development of their relationship is, as Susan insists, marriage, but this presents Parker with a major problem. If he marries Spenser off, how can he avoid the difficulties Chandler encountered when he decided to have Philip Marlowe marry Linda Loring. Happily, Susan saves Spenser (and Parker) from a confining domestic arrangement by declining his proposal. She knows he cannot give up his profession and move to a quiet little house in Smithfield, nor is she willing to leave the community where she has lived for twenty years. Nevertheless, Spenser has come to accept her view of their relationship, a decision prompted largely by his involvement with the Shepards. Susan saves him from marriage by being satisfied merely with his proposal.

In addition to the Shepards' marriage, Parker provides another revealing mirror for Spenser in the character of Hawk, a tall imposing black man whom he encounters at Harv's house when he first arrives in Hyannis to begin looking for Pam. Hawk's presence warns Spenser that Shepard is in serious trouble. Spenser has known Hawk for twenty years, since the time they trained together and boxed on the same fight card. Their verbal banter attests to a relationship that has developed out of long-term familiarity. But wherever Hawk is, something is amiss, for Spenser knows he is a notorious enforcer for the mob.

The two mirror each other interestingly. Both have but a single name. Both are free-lance, choosing only the work they enjoy. Both are men of honor, men of their word. (Hawk "won't say *yes* and do *no*," says Spenser admiringly.) Both maintain an independent relationship with their employers: when King Powers orders Hawk to kill Spenser after he learns that he arranged the bogus gun deal, Hawk declines: "Naw, I don't guess I am going to do what I'm told. I think I'm going to leave that up to you, boss," he says, exhibiting the same streak of insubordination that got Spenser kicked out of the District Attorney's office years earlier. But when Hawk insists too much on their similarities, Spenser insists on their differences. Hawk, you see, fashions himself a "soldier of fortune," but Spenser knows he is nothing more than a muscle-and-gun man, a legbreaker for the mob.

Susan attempts to distinguish between the two by arguing that while Spenser aims to help people, Hawk hurts them. Hawk reminds her that maybe Spenser aims to help, but "he also like the work. You know? I mean he could be a social worker if he just want to help . . . Just don't be so sure me and old Spenser are so damn different, Susan." Maybe Hawk is right, maybe Spenser is more interested in demonstrating his skill by rescuing people from dangerous situations than in the individuals themselves. Maybe Hawk is right when he says to Spenser, "maybe you a lot more like me than you want to say."

In Parker's two previous novels, Susan played the role of moral sounding board for Spenser, a surrogate conscience against which he could evaluate the ethics of his actions. The questions she raises about his actions force him constantly to reexamine the morality of his behavior. In *Promised Land*, Hawk plays a reverse role; he is a dramatic reminder to Spenser that if he isn't careful, the distinctions he labors so hard to maintain between himself and Hawk will disappear. The key to the differentiation between the two is Spenser's moral conscience, his awareness of the ethical implications of his actions. Hawk states the difference more simply: "You complicate your life, Spenser. You think about things too much." "That's one of the things that makes me not you," Spenser points out, and as long as he continues to consider the ethics of a situation, he can prevent himself from becoming too Hawk-like. But he cannot always easily maintain that distinction. In *Mortal Stakes*, for example, he found himself in a situation that resulted in his killing two men, an action which disturbed him deeply. But in *Promised Land*, he delivers a whole crew of criminals to the police in order to save the marriage of two felons he doesn't particularly like, and it doesn't seem to bother him much at all.

Hawk and Spenser represent opposite ways of acting upon the perception of one's freedom. Both are loners working on the fringes of society, often outside its prescribed laws. But Hawk's exercise of his freedom in the service of gangsters and to the detriment of people like Harv Shepard who are stupid enough to get involved with him provides one measure by which Spenser can establish his limits and maintain his integrity. Just as his involvement with the Shepards' marital problems teaches him something about the inadequacy of his relationship with Susan, his awareness of Hawk teaches him something about himself, about the need to be constantly alert to the morality of a situation before acting. In a way, Spenser needs a character like Hawk around and so, just before the police are about to spring their trap, he warns Hawk who slips away unnoticed. Hawk later repays the favor by refusing Powers' order to kill Spenser. Hawk, still insisting on the professional similarities between them, reasons, "There ain't all that many of us left, guys like old Spenser and me. He was gone there'd be one less."

The title of the novel provides a clue to its theme, one which it shares with many Chandler and Macdonald novels, indeed with any number of American novels—the disappointment that arises from unfulfilled dreams and false promises. Pam and Harv Shepard met in college, married right after graduation (both graduated from Colby College in 1954, the same year Parker did), and settled down to a life they were led to believe would be happy ever after. Harv worked hard at his land development business, Pam raised the kids in their fashionable Hyannis home. To all appearances, they had attained the American Dream. But something went wrong, for their success didn't bring happiness. Harv could never stop panting after more success, which he measured in dollars. Inevitably, he becomes overextended and has to borrow from King Powers (at 3.5% interest weekly) to cover up his manipulation of escrow funds. His whole world begins to crumble when first his wife leaves and then Hawk shows up to demand payment of the borrowed money.

Harv is the latest variation of a type of character that appears with great frequency in Parker's fiction—the husband and father who cannot separate work from play, who is so caught up in his work that he ignores his family, depriving them of the important things the money he accumulates can never purchase. In *The Godwulf Manuscript*, it was Roland Orchard's marriage to his job that led to his daughter's rejection of his life-style, a rejection that resulted in her involvement in radical campus activities. In *God Save the Child*, it is Roger Bartlett's absorption in his work that causes his son to seek a surrogate father in the person of Vic Harroway. Harv Shepard is too busy to notice his wife's unhappiness, and one can only wonder about the future of his surly daughter, Millie, who dismisses her father as a jerk because all he talks about is money and business. In *Three Weeks in Spring*, Parker reveals that he leaves his work at the office, never writing at home in the evenings or on weekends; he admits to being resentful of any intrusion of work into family life. The only male character who is an exception to the type (and the character Spenser identifies with most) is Marty Rabb in *Mortal Stakes*. Rabb's wife tells Spenser that unless she has seen the game, she doesn't know if he has won or lost when he comes home because he does not allow his professional life to intrude upon his family. Marty has his problems, but they are not family problems and do not arise from his failures either as husband or father.

Pam shares with her husband the same dreams of success, but she too discovers that there is no perfect bliss in the promised land. She knows Harv loves her and provides the things she wants, but she also knows she isn't happy. One symptom of her unhappiness is her frigidity; unable to have sex with her husband, she is driven to a series of one-night affairs in an attempt to resolve her sexual problems. The next step is running away entirely, although she has no idea where she is going. All she knows for certain is that the life she was living was a far cry from the "happily ever after" life she felt was promised to her, and she wants something more.

An important conversation occurs between Pam and Spenser as they look at the Boston skyline from an observatory outside the city. The view of the buildings in the distance excites Pam, and she wonders why the scene seems so romantic. Spenser suggests it is because the buildings are filled with promise: "From a distance they promise everything, whatever you're after. They look clean and permanent against the sky like that. Up close you notice dog litter around the foundations." He warns her that if she spends all her time looking up at the spires, she won't see the dog litter until it is too late and she steps in it. Pam gets the message: "Into each life some shit must fall?" she asks. Pam and Harv have focused too narrowly on the romantic promises of the future and consequently were unprepared for the messes they would inevitably step in along the way. "They ran after the wrong promise and got into things they couldn't control," is the way Spenser describes their plight to the police in explaining why he feels they are basically harmless people who deserve a second chance.

Several details in the novel underscore Parker's view that the Shepards' problem is essentially their childish response to their situation. For example, the book Susan is reading during her stay on the Cape with Spenser is entitled *Children of the Dream*. What better subtitle for *Promised Land* than this, for the Shepards are truly children of the American Dream, inheritors, they hope, of all its promise. What they must do to save themselves, Spenser might argue, is grow up, learn to deal with their unhappiness in a mature way. Pam reminds Spenser of the character in Frost's "Mending Wall" who "will not go behind his father's saying." It is one thing for a fifteen-year-old like Kevin Bartlett to run away from home in search of happines, but something quite different for a forty-three-year-old woman like Pam Shepard. A child's response is inappropriate for an adult, who must learn that it is immature to expect that all the wonderful promises made in childhood will be fulfilled in adulthood. On the walls of the observatory from which they view the Boston skyline, Spenser notices some graffiti spray-painted remarks, one of which is about the sister of someone named Mangan. Given Parker's propensity for literary allusion, it is entirely possible that he has in mind here James Joyce's "Araby," a story about a young boy's infatuation with the sister of his friend Mangan. The story depicts the boy's romantic desire to demonstrate his love for the older girl by bringing her a gift from Araby, a local bazaar. He is so consumed by infatuation that he invests the bazaar in his mind with such romantic promise that it becomes for him the symbol of his romantic quest. When he arrives at the bazaar, however, it is closing for the night and he sees it for what it really is—a tawdry, cheap affair. Disappointed and angry with himself, he begins to weep. Joyce's touching theme about the painful lesson that growing up requires the shedding of unrealistic fantasies applies directly to *Promised Land*. Like the boy in "Araby," the Shepards have invested the future with a romantic promise that is unrealistic and unrealizable; but disappointment (which inevitably comes) does not mean the end of the world. The lesson may cause grief, but it is necessary, an important step in the process of maturing. Spenser demonstrated in *Mortal Stakes* his commitment to the notion that one can overcome the mistakes of the past, as Linda Rabb did, and still attain a happy life. The Shepards put that belief to a real test, but by his efforts on their behalf, despite his ambivalent feelings about the couple and his awareness of the seriousness of their mistakes, Spenser reaffirms his conviction.

Harv Shepard's belief that the way to insure his wife's continuing love for him and the way to demonstrate his worth to her (and to himself) is by accumulating material possessions evokes another literary parallel—it reminds us of the tragic mistake Jay Gatsby made in confusing means and ends by allowing his pursuit of wealth to blind himself to the reality of his goal, Daisy Buchanan. *Promised Land* echoes *The Great Gatsby* in several ways. Both Gatsby and Shepard live in beautiful, expensive houses on the ocean, and both mistake the tangible evidence of wealth as the key to happiness. Nick Carraway's final comment on Gatsby's relentless pursuit of a future that keeps receding before him could serve as a warning to Shepard: "It eluded us then, but that's no matter— tomorrow we will run faster, stretch out our arms farther . . . And one fine morning—" Both Gatsby and Shepard become figures in a larger design. Gatsby's failure represents the failure of the American Dream which Fitzgerald symbolized in his novel by the transformation of the "green breast of the new world," which the early Dutch sailors saw as the promise of America, into the ugly dust heaps that line the road between East Egg and New York. *Promised Land* has its own symbol of failure—the "bulldozed wasteland" that is all that remains of the urban renewal projects that Spenser passes on his way from Cape Cod to New Bedford. At New Bedford, Spenser looks out over the ocean at a depressing sight: "Oil slick, cigarette wrappers, dead fish, gelatinous-looking pieces of water-soaked driftwood, an unraveled condom looking like an eel skin against the coffee-colored water." He wonders if it could have looked like this when Herman Melville shipped out from New Bedford on a whaler one hundred and thirty years ago. "Christ, I hope not," he mutters disgustedly.

As he did in *God Save the Child,* Parker again provides a bifocal view of America, with the contrast between past and present carrying the same satiric message it did in the earlier novel—the American Dream has become tarnished by progress, greed, and misuse. As Spenser drives along the Cape toward Hyannis, he sees pines and maples and, from time to time, the ocean in the bright morning sun; but before long, the natural beauty of the view gives way to the McDonald's, Holiday Inns, shopping centers, and the like and he concludes that if Bartholomew Gosnold (the English explorer who first named Cape Cod) had approached from this direction, he would have kept going. Like Fitzgerald's Dutch sailors (or like Squanto, whom Spenser mentions in *God Save the Child*), Gosnold would be saddened at the present-day reality of the promise of the past, at how tawdry the landscape has become. "Promised Land" has been reduced to nothing more than the name Shepard gives to the housing development he is promoting, one which significantly rests precariously on embezzled funds. Another damaging contrast between past and present can be found in the scene at Plimouth Plantation, the site where the first European colonists settled in Massachusetts. What was for them the place where they hoped to attain their dream of a new world becomes in *Promised Land* the setting where Spenser and Pam Shepard meet to plan her escape from a robbery and murder charge. One is reminded here of the association between Gatsby and Meyer Wolfsheim, the gambler whose fixing of the 1919 World Series was used by Fitzgerald to symbolize the pervasive corruption which had reached into even the most cherished of American symbols. In

Promised Land, even the Pilgrims are tainted by the corruption of the modern world.

One cannot overlook the weaknesses in plot and the frequently inert quality of *Promised Land.* One reason for the latter problem is that, despite Spenser's appeal to Susan that "You really ought to watch what I do, and, pretty much, I think, you'll know what I am," more of his character is revealed through exposition, less through action, in this novel than in any of the others. Although the pace of the first third of the novel is brisk, the narrative lags when the plot becomes complicated by Pam's involvement in the bank robbery, and it drifts off into lengthy discursive eddies. The novel would be unquestionably improved by the elimination of several conversations between Spenser and Pam, and between Spenser and Susan. At their best, such discussions serve to clarify some aspect of Spenser's character, or prompt him to assess his behavior in the light of Susan's probing questions; at their worst, they are merely repetitious statements of Spenser's code or simply occasions for embarassing flattery of him. Parker is much more effective in revealing Spenser's character through action and narrative style. When he depends too much on talk, as he does in *Promised Land,* the novel suffers. There is also a notable decline in Parker's interest in secondary characters: Rose and Jane, Pam's two feminist colleagues, for example, are never fully realized as characters. More serious a problem is the sketchiness with which the Shepard family is portrayed. Not only do we see just one of the Shepard children in the novel, Parker appears confused by even the *number* of children: three children are mentioned throughout the book, but at the end, as Shepard begs for his life from King Powers, he says he has *four* kids.

On the other hand, one should not underestimate Parker's success in incorporating personal drama, psychological insight, and social commentary into a serious exploration of contemporary American values. *Promised Land* echoes Fitzgerald's *The Great Gatsby* in its embodiment of a vision of America in the story of its characters and echoes Chandler's *The Long Goodbye* in its use of the detective novel for a serious examination of character, especially the character of the hero. And despite the problems with secondary characters, the main characters are vividly portrayed. Susan Silverman continues to grow as a character and as an influence on Spenser, and the introduction of Hawk adds a new dimension to the novel. Not only is he an interesting character in his own right, his role as foil to Spenser offers Parker a new way of defining his hero's character. That Parker has not exhausted the possibilities of Hawk is shown by his return appearance in the next Spenser novel, *The Judas Goat*.

Mortal Stakes demonstrated that Parker could successfully combine the elements of good mystery writing—plot, pacing, mystery, suspense—with such literary techniques as three-dimensional characterization, symbolism, and imagery to produce a serious and compelling exploration of theme. The failure of *Promised Land* to repeat that success proves how difficult it is to accomplish the task and illustrates all too clearly that once the delicate balance between theme and action is upset in a mystery novel, the work as a whole suffers.

THE JUDAS GOAT

The Judas Goat (1978) is a novel with enough action, adventure, and suspense to suggest that Parker was aware of the flaws that weakened *Promised Land*. He sought to avoid them in his new novel by emphasizing what the earlier novel lacked—action—and by returning to those elements with which he had demonstrated his greatest skill—vivid characterization and witty dialogue. Spenser is summoned to the home of millionaire Hugh Dixon, who seeks to hire him to avenge the deaths of his wife and two teenage daughters, killed as a result of a terrorist bombing in a London restaurant the previous year. Dixon himself was critically wounded, spent a year in the hospital, and is now paralyzed, unable to undertake the job himself. Spenser insists he doesn't do assassinations, but out of sympathy for Dixon he agrees to take the job. (He is also interested in the fee—$2500 for each terrorist, $25,000 for the lot; Spenser admits to being down to his last $237; and Dixon says "a hungry Captain Midnight is just what I need.") So Spenser heads for London.

He places an advertisement in the London *Times* offering a reward of one thousand pounds for information about the bombing. After a nervous week of waiting, the ad produces dramatic results— Spenser discovers two gunmen waiting in his hotel room to ambush him. Before they can shoot him, however, he kills both of them. The following day, two more gunmen appear outside his room, and he disarms both. All four turn out to be members of the terrorist group he is after. He decides he could use some help with the remaining terrorists, so he arranges for his old friend (and sometime antagonist) Hawk, who played an important role in *Promised Land,* to join him in London. He also gets valuable assistance from Kathie Caldwell, the sole female member of the terrorists, who unwittingly acts as his Judas goat, leading him and Hawk from London to Copenhagen and finally to Denmark. After a series of bloody encounters, they kill or capture all nine members of the terrorist group Liberty, which is dedicated to maintaining white dominance in Africa. Spenser also uncovers a new plot, this one involving the assassination of African medal winners at the Olympic games being held in Montreal. Spenser, Hawk, and their Judas goat-cum-associate Kathie head for Canada in time to disrupt the plot and prevent the assassinations. At the end of the novel, all nine terrorists have been rounded up (although Spenser frees Kathie), Liberty has been put out of business, and another bloody terrorist act has been prevented. Dixon is so pleased with Spenser that he doubles his fee, paying him $50,000.

Even a brief synopsis such as this reveals some significant differences between *The Judas Goat* and the previous Spenser books. For one thing, the novel is, strictly speaking, not a mystery novel— there is nothing for Spenser to solve. Instead he must use his considerable skill and ingenuity to locate the terrorists (whose faces he knows from sketches the police provide) and deliver them, dead or alive, to the authorities. Consequently, the focus is on suspense and adventure, not mystery. Also, Parker abandons his usual Boston setting for such colorful places as London, Amsterdam, Copenhagen, and Montreal. This not only gives him an opportunity to describe fresh locations, but more importantly it prohibits him from developing specifically American themes, as he did in *God Save the*

Child and *Promised Land*. The change is significant because virtually every hard-boiled novel is set in America, which is not surprising since the genre is of American origin. The opportunity to comment on American social and cultural values is also a feature that attracts many writers to the field. Nevertheless, Spenser doesn't seem at all out of place in Europe, perhaps because his character is fundamentally more cosmopolitan and more sociable than many of his fictional colleagues. (One has difficulty, for example, imagining Philip Marlowe in Copenhagen.) Parker doesn't totally relinquish his interest in social issues, however, for *The Judas Goat* obviously makes a strong indictment against terrorism, especially against those radical groups which display so little concern for human life that they have no compunction about tossing a bomb into a crowded restaurant where innocent people are likely to be hurt or killed. However, this is not the kind of complex issue that demands elaborate development, since senseless killing of innocent victims is hardly a morally ambiguous matter. Such actions might be defensible to the terrorists, but to Spenser they are nothing less than cold-blooded murder and he is therefore untroubled by the distinct possibility he might have to kill one or more of them.

Parker also eliminates many of the symbolic layers that emcumbered the action of some of his previous novels, especially *Promised Land*, and this, coupled with a determined shift in emphasis from mystery to action, achieves his goal of refocusing attention on Spenser. Despite his claim to Pam Shepard that if she wishes to understand his character, she should watch his actions, Spenser's actions are all too infrequent in *Promised Land*. By placing Spenser back in the center of the action, and by calling upon him to act frequently, Parker allows the reader to do exactly what Spenser wishes, i.e., judge his character through his actions.

One clue to Parker's intention in *The Judas Goat* is the book Spenser mentions (three times) he is reading, *Regeneration Through Violence* by Richard Slotkin, an exhaustive and penetrating analysis of the same subject Parker dealt with in his dissertation—the frontier myth and the various archetypes in American legend (e.g., Daniel Boone, Davy Crockett) and literature (e.g., Natty Bumppo) which embody qualities of the mythical American hero, virtues originally associated with the taming of the wilderness. Slotkin argues that since myth is extended metaphor rather than abstract conceptualization, the most effective myths are those in which action becomes symbolic, where it provides the key to character: e.g., the contrast between the action of Natty Bumppo in civilization and his behavior in the wilderness imparts valuable information about his character. Parker clearly endorses Slotkin's thesis, and the frequent references to his book in *The Judas Goat* hint at Parker's resolve to use action as the key to Spenser's character, utilizing it as an effective corrective to the inertia of *Promised Land*. The result is a novel that comes closer than any of his others to accomplishing what those works he discussed in his dissertation do—embody through action certain characteristics of the archetypal American hero.

Spenser's initial test occurs after he has arrived in London, settled in the Mayfair hotel, and placed an ad in the newspaper offering a reward for information about the restaurant bombing. He includes his address and waits for an answer. For six days, nothing happens. Then a letter is left at the desk for him. The cat and mouse game begins, for Spenser assumes (correctly) that the desk is being watched as he accepts the letter and realizes that his identity is now known to whoever is watching. He leaves the hotel and spots a woman he noticed in the hotel lobby following him. He returns to his room to set a trap by sprinkling some talcum powder on the floor just inside the door which will leave a telltale mark should anyone enter his room. Later, returning to his room, he notices a faint talcum powder footprint in the hall outside his door. He carefully unlocks the door, pushes it open, and quickly moves aside. Nothing happens. Certain that someone is in his room, he waits patiently in the hall. Whoever has the greater endurance and the steelier nerves will win the encounter. At one point he considers calling hotel security, but decides against it, knowing that the first person through the door will be shot, and he accepts as his the responsibility for this situation. Finally, after several hours, a man rushes from the room and fires at Spenser, missing him. Spenser shoots him and then dashes into the room, where a second gunman wounds him in the thigh, but Spenser manages to kill him before he can shoot again. He has outwitted and outwaited the two (both of whom he identifies from the police sketches as members of the terrorist group), and has demonstrated his superior skill and patience. Two down, seven to go.

Inspector Downes of the London police is understandably unhappy with the messy scene Spenser has created in his room and reminds him, "We can't have you running around London shooting down suspected anarchists at random and collecting the bounty." Downes has a valid point, but he is also a bit miffed at Spenser for accomplishing what the London authorities have been unable to do for a year—locate the terrorists. Spenser reminds Downes that he acted in self-defense: "I don't shoot people I don't have to shoot. I'm here doing a job that needs to be done, that you people are too busy to do. These two clowns tried to kill me, remember. I didn't shoot them because they were suspected anarchists. I shot them to keep them from shooting me." Downes remains unconvinced and reminds Spenser rather sarcastically that each dead terrorist will buy him "half an inexpensive car." Spenser is unquestionably being well-paid, but the fact remains he will be paid whether the terrorists are killed or simply delivered to the authorities, and he is also performing dangerous work, his vulnerability attested to by the wound in his thigh (or, as his doctor corrects him, in the "arse"). Like the archetypal American hero in the wilderness, Spenser's tests of virtue gain added significance when they involve the element of personal risk. A quote Parker included in his dissertation from Mark Spilka's essay on Ernest Hemingway is appropriate here. Spilka, commenting on Hemingway's fascination with death, noted that "The risk of death lends moral seriousness to a code which lacks it. The risk is arbitrary; when a man elects to meet it, his beliefs take on subjective weight and he is able to give meaning to his private life." Although Spenser may not consciously seek out life-threatening situations, he is engaged in a profession where danger is an integral element, and each time he proves himself in a test involving physical danger, he authenticates his code of behavior and, by extension, himself.

His next test occurs the following day when, as he is walking down the hall toward his hotel room, he notices a suspicious man in the corridor. Wary of another ambush, he strolls past his room and glances back in time to see a second man peering from behind the stairway door. He continues to the service elevator, takes it up three floors, gets off and, in his bare feet, heads silently down the stairs like a deerhunter stalking his prey. The challenge here is to disarm the man without shooting him (which he could easily do). He succeeds, surprising the man from behind, knocking him out, and taking his gun. Then he opens the door, walks down the hall and, as he passes the other man, pulls his coat down over his arms, trapping his gun hand in his pocket. As he pushes him into his room, the man pulls a knife and wounds Spenser in the cheek. Spenser knocks the knife away, dislocating the man's elbow in the process. Terrorists number three and four are now accounted for (although the man on the stairwell has disappeared by the time Spenser returns to collect him). Inspector Downes is, as one might expect, equally displeased at this second incident in two days and offers another disparaging comment about Spenser earning another half a car. He also suggests that perhaps Spenser could use some help. Spenser is smart enough to know he has stumbled onto something big, and so decides to hire Hawk as his associate.

It turns out that Hawk renders assistance to both Spenser and Parker. By joining forces, Spenser and Hawk are able to dispose of the remaining terrorists, but Hawk's role is more than a Tonto to Spenser's Lone Ranger. He resumes the role he played in *Promised Land*, that of foil to Spenser, a sometimes clear, sometimes refracted image of his character. But he does more than this. He is, for example, a source of much of the humor in the book. Hawk is anything but a comic character, but his conversations with Spenser are frequently entertaining. In *Mortal Stakes* and *Promised Land*, Parker depended almost exclusively on Susan Silverman for witty conversation with Spenser, but the problem that presents is that, by virtue of their relationship, the tenor of the wit is largely sexual. Hawk introduces new areas of humorous dialogue. For example, when he tells Spenser that he has of late been living with a female Harvard professor, Spenser wonders, "How'd you get along with her seeing-eye dog." And when Hawk lapses into his slave jargon, Spenser reminds him that he ought to "can that Aunt Jemima crap" because he is as much a "down-home darkie as Truman Capote."

Aside from their banter, however, the significant feature of their relationship is, as it was in *Promised Land*, the parallels (and significant differences) between them. Both men adhere to a code of behavior, but they play the game with different rules; Hawk follows rules but, unlike Spenser, never allows his feelings to intrude. When Spenser questions whether Hawk has *any* rules, he replies, "I just got fewer than you. And I ain't softhearted. But you know, I say I gonna do something, I do it. It gets done. I hire on for something, I stay hired. I do what I take the bread for." Spenser usually ends up doing more than he is hired to do while Hawk, by contrast, does *only* what he is hired to do. When at the end of the novel Dixon doubles his fee, Spenser offers half, $25,000, to Hawk, who refuses because it would complicate his simple rules: he agreed to do a job for $150 a day, he did the job, he will accept nothing more than the agreed-upon amount. Hawk reminds Spenser that what he said about him in *Promised Land* still applies—he complicates his life too much by feeling and sentiment. When Hawk arrives in London and listens to Spenser explain how they will approach the terrorists, he asks, "Why not go the easy route and whack 'em right off?" Spenser is as prepared for violence as Hawk, but *his* code demands that it be provoked by the enemy; as he explained to Downes, he will not kill the terrorists if he has a choice. Hawk ridicules this needlessly cautious attitude, appreciating as he does the efficiency of shooting first and asking questions later. This, of course, crystalizes the significant difference between them: Hawk has no conscience and refuses to permit feelings to get in his way. Spenser wonders if Hawk *has* any feelings, remarking to Susan that in the twenty years he has known Hawk, he has never seen him happy, sad, elated, anything. He is machinelike in his efficiency. And his coldness.

This crucial distinction between Hawk and Spenser is best exemplified by their contrasting attitudes toward Kathie Caldwell after she is delivered into their custody by Paul, the leader of the terrorist group. They must figure out what to do with her. Spenser decides to trust her and take her with them to Montreal where she, out of gratitude, loyalty, lust, or whatever, offers herself to him. He refuses, unwilling to take advantage of her, among other reasons. Hawk, on the other hand, has no qualms about enjoying her sexual favors when she turns her attention to him, but he also would have no hesitation in killing her. Spenser knows that if Hawk were on his own, he would have dropped her in a canal rather than take her with them. At the end of the novel Spenser, in appreciation of her role in stopping Paul's plan, allows Kathie to go free, telling Dixon she was not one of the nine killers. Hawk is disgusted. "Sentimental, dumb," is his response. There is absolutely no room for emotion in Hawk's system. He cannot even understand why Spenser feels an obligation to keep Dixon informed of their plans. When Spenser explains he owes it to him, that he's got nothing else that matters, Hawk remarks sourly, "You and Ann Landers, babe. Everybody's trouble." Hawk does his job, no more, no less. He does it efficiently, but with no thought of morality, compassion, or mercy. In many respects—his amorality, his lack of sentiment, his ruthlessness, his single-minded dedication to his job—Hawk comes much closer than Spenser does to the original conception of the hard-boiled detective as he emerged in the early *Black Mask* stories, especially to a character like Hammett's Continental Op. The contrast between Hawk and Spenser illustrates just how much the hard-boiled hero has softened in his various manifestations over the years. Hawk also reminds us that there is much more to admire in a hero than blind strength, ruthless efficiency, and brute force. If the private eye is an embodiment of the reader's fantasies (and he is), then a hero like Spenser represents something more valuable than Hawk does—he sets an example not only for how one would like to think one *might* act, but also for how one *ought* to act.

Hawk gets an opportunity to prove his real worth to Spenser in Copenhagen, where they have followed the terrorists' trail. Spenser is captured by three of the terrorists while watching Kathie's apartment and brought inside, where he meets Paul, the leader of Liberty, who confers with Kathie in the adjoining room about what to do with him. Suddenly, Hawk bursts into the room, shotgun blazing, and kills the three men guarding Spenser. With his usual efficiency and his direct, uncomplicated approach, Hawk rescues Spenser from what appears to be certain death. Terrorists four, five, and six are now accounted for, but in the confusion Paul and Kathie escape. The only lead Spenser has is an Amsterdam address he copied from some letters he found in Kathie's London apartment, so off to the Netherlands the two go. Nothing happens there until, returning to their hotel room one evening, they hear a muffled sound inside. Entering cautiously, they discover Kathie bound and gagged on the bed and the remaining two terrorists dead on the floor. Pinned to Kathie is a note from Paul explaining that he de-livered the remaining terrorists to Spenser to get him off his back because, as he writes, "We have much to do and you are in the way."

Spenser's job is finished, all nine terrorists have been rounded up, seven of them killed. And yet he is unsatisfied, worried about Lib-erty's next move. Kathie confesses she does not know Paul's plan but remembers he mentioned something about the Olympic games, which have just begun in Montreal. Spenser, dissatisified with "only the leaves of the crabgrass," wants Paul, "the root." If he were motivated only by money, he would stop here and collect his $25,000 from Dixon. But he has never been one to leave unfinished business: "I have the end of something and I want to pull it all the way out of its hole before I quit." He sees an opportunity to prevent another terrorist act which might injure innocent people like the Dixons. So, accompanied by Hawk and Kathie, Spenser heads for Montreal although he has nothing more concrete to go on than his suspicion that Paul might be planning some action during the Olympic games.

Using Dixon's influence, they obtain tickets to the games in order to move freely through the grandstand looking for Paul and his accomplice, Zachary. Spenser knows what Paul looks like, and Kathie promises they will have little trouble recognizing Zachary because of his size—he is six-feet-seven and weighs more than three hundred pounds. Once again, Spenser's hunch pays off: Paul practically bumps into him while he is eating a hot dog. He follows him to the third deck and watches as he selects a narrow space next to a washroom, takes out what looks to be a spyglass, carefully focuses on the field, places a mark on the wall, and then leaves. Spenser concludes that Paul was lining up in his sight the location of the awards platform in order to shoot an athlete (most likely from one of the African nations) during the awards ceremony. He watches the spot carefully for three days, waiting for something to happen. Finally, Paul and Zachary return. When Paul removes a high-powered rifle from his equipment bag, Spenser decides it is time for him and Hawk to act. Hawk moves in and knocks Paul unconscious with the butt of his gun, and then he and Spenser face off against the enormous Zachary.

Spenser has fought tough opponents before, including Vic Harroway, the former Mr. Northeastern America, in *God Save the Child*, but he has never faced anyone quite like Zachary, who is gargantuan; Spenser notes wryly that he "was nowhere near as big as an elephant. In fact he wasn't much bigger than a Belgian draught horse." Spenser and Hawk are both big men, but Zachary easily disarms them, pushes them aside, and flees the stadium with the two in pursuit. He is surprisingly agile for a big man ("very fast for a guy the size of a drive-in movie" is the way Spenser puts it), but

they finally reach him and, like Davy Crockett braving a bear in the
forest, they face off in a decisive test of strength and courage.
(Zachary is even described in bearlike terms: "Slightly ahead of us,
slightly above, with the sun behind him, he stood and waited, high
and huge, as if he had risen on his hind legs. We had bayed him.")
The ensuing fight is the most brutal that Spenser has been in, but
he and Hawk finally defeat the mighty Zachary. Spenser suffers a
broken nose (his sixth) and a fractured arm, but his pain is diminished considerably by the knowledge that he has prevented Paul
and Zachary from carrying out their bloody plan. Furthermore,
since Zachary isn't one of the original nine terrorists Dixon hired
him to find, he belongs to Spenser, who enjoys a measure of personal satisfaction at having performed this job on his own initiative.

Spenser faces a greater number of tests of skill and endurance
in this novel than in any of the previous ones. Some are physical,
especially the hand-to-hand battle with Zachary, and each requires
that he demonstrate his fitness to meet the special demands of his
profession. Some call upon other skills—ingenuity, for example, in
anticipating the first ambush on him in his hotel, or stealth in de-
fusing the second. Also, his self-confidence and patience are frequently tested, either as he spends hours outside his room waiting
for the gunmen inside to make the first move, or as he waits day
after day for a response to his newspaper ad. Parker noted wistfully
in his dissertation that, for all practical purposes, there is no longer
any wilderness one can escape to in order to test oneself. But the
nature of the private eye's dangerous profession provides him with
situations that call upon those same strengths and virtues demanded
in a previous age of such legendary heroes as Daniel Boone and
Natty Bumppo, thereby allowing him an opportunity to justify his
code and validate his worth.

Frequent references in the novel to popular heroes of the
American West—Paladin, Matt Dillon, Shane—also remind us of
the kinship between the Western hero and the private eye, especially
as both embody the deerslayer archetype that Cooper and other
nineteenth-century writers developed. One Western reference, however, suggests a different analogy. While spending the evening
with Susan, Spenser finds himself watching (for the sixth or seventh
time) on television *The Magnificent Seven*, a remake of Akira
Kurosawa's classic film, *The Seven Samurai*. The two films demon-

strate the close parallels that exist between the Western hero and the traditional Japanese samurai warrior. Although Spenser's roots are predominantly American, one line of his ancestry can be traced back through the Western hero to the samurai warrior, revealing certain generic similarities such as courage, commitment, strength, loyalty, as well as those virtues associated with Bushido, the samurai's code: learning, self-control, honor. The reference to *The Magnificent Seven* reminds us that the archetypal foundations of the American private eye have something of an international flavor to them.

In the character of Kathie Caldwell, Spenser's Judas goat, Parker paints an interesting psychosexual portrait of a beautiful woman whose stylishly attractive appearance belies her ruthless terrorist inclinations. When he follows her, Spenser concentrates on her more alluring features: her blond hair, buxom figure, high quality thighs, and "free, long-striding, hip-swing walk with a lot of spring to it." But when he breaks into her London apartment and searches it carefully, some revealing facts about her personality emerge. Her apartment is immaculate, with everything from the shoes in the closet to the books on the wall arranged in perfect order. Also, the apartment is decorated entirely in black and white— even the clothes in the closet are in shades of black, white, or grey— and all the furnishings are made of plastic or stainless steel. The picture one gets is of a compulsively orderly and repressed personality with little or no feeling or emotion. However, a locked drawer in her bedroom bureau reveals another side to her personality: Spenser discovers twelve pairs of French string bikini underpants in a rainbow of colors, as well as lace bras, a black garter belt, and black fishnet stockings. In a secret compartment behind the underwear, he also uncovers a cache of pistols, ammunition, and hand grenades. Beneath that controlled and repressed exterior is a terrorist killer and sexual tigress.

The latter quality is dramatically revealed to Spenser when he and Hawk discover her in their hotel room bound to the bed alongside the two dead terrorists Paul has delivered. As Hawk proceeds to untie her, she goes into a frenzy, arching her back, thrusting her pelvis forward, gasping, "I'm bound and helpless, shall you tear my clothing, use me, degrade me, drive me mad?" Rape fantasies—or at least sexually submissive ones—apparently figure prominently in Kathie's psyche. Now having been abandoned by Paul, her leader and lover, she quickly transfers her allegiance to Spenser and agrees to accompany him to Montreal. There they rent an apartment, where one evening Kathie appears in Spenser's bedroom, stark naked, and offers herself to him, climbs all over him, begs him to "do with me what you will." Spenser struggles to control himself and suggests she needs to "find some other way to relate with people." Kathie's naked assault of Spenser reminds us of the equally naked and equally neurotic assault on Marlowe by Carmen Sternwood in *The Big Sleep*. Like Marlowe, Spenser refuses because he judges Kathie to be unpredictable, perhaps dangerous. But also, as he made clear to Pam Shepard in *Promised Land*, he has chosen to remain faithful to Susan.

Susan analyzes Kathie's behavior for Spenser: "She needs a master. She needs structure. When you destroyed her structure, and her master turned her out, she latched on to you. When she wanted to solidify the relationship by complete submission, which for her must be sexual, you turned her out." She explains Kathie's odd sexual behavior as an extension of her rigid and repressed personality: "She finds some connection between sex and helplessness and helplessness and humiliation and humiliation and pleasure." Parker's intent is not to trace the roots of terrorism to sexual neuroses, but Susan's analysis of Kathie helps to explain her presence as the only woman in the terrorist group. Moreover, in her search for structure she can be viewed as simply a more dramatic version of the typical Parker character—such as Terry Orchard, Kevin Bartlett, Marge Bartlett, Pam Shepard—who is desperately seeking to fill an emotional void. Kathie's needs are just more neurotic and the satisfaction she seeks more extreme than Parker's other characters. (One can trace in Parker's novels an increasingly destructive pattern in the solutions his characters find, beginning with Terry Orchard, whose search led her to involvement with a radical campus group responsible for the theft of a manuscript, becoming more serious with Kevin Bartlett's extortion of money from his parents and Pam Shepard's thoughtless participation in armed robbery and murder, culminating in Kathie Caldwell's active participation in terrorist activities which cause the death of innocent victims.)

The Judas Goat is an important novel for Parker not only because it shows his willingness to attempt new departures—placing Spenser in a foreign setting, for example; but also because in it he takes measures—more action, sharper characterizations, increased dosages of ironic humor—to correct the drift that marred *Promised Land*. The ironic humor, for example, prevents Spenser from taking himself too seriously (which he tended to do in *Promised Land*). As he stands in the corridor waiting what seems an eternity for the gunmen in his room to make a move, he notices his hand beginning to fall asleep and starts to worry, imagining what the scene in heaven would be like if he got killed because his gun hand fell asleep:

> How'd you get shot, Spenser? Well, it's this way, Saint Pete, I was staked out in a hotel corridor but my hand went to sleep. Then after a while my entire body nodded off. Did Bogey's hand ever go to sleep, Spenser? Did Kerry Drake's? No, sir. I don't think we can admit you here to Private-Eye Heaven, Spenser.

Later, after killing the two men, he notices his heart pumping furiously and concludes wryly, "I'm not gonna get shot, I'm gonna have cardiac arrest some day." And when the messenger who brings the tickets to the Olympic games asks to check his identification and, looking at Spenser's picture on his license, says, "Yeah, . . that's you," Spenser replies, "It disappoints me too." Such instances of self-deprecating humor, coupled with Spenser's quick-witted jests with Hawk and typically good-natured sexual banter with Susan, give the novel a liveliness that was notably lacking in *Promised Land*. Moreover, the whole narrative style is as crisp and invigorating as anything Parker has written. He even makes those scenes where Spenser stands around waiting for something to happen interesting to read.

What emerges most vividly from a reading of Parker's novels is the singularly engaging figure of Spenser, who continues to evolve in interesting ways. He remains essentially the same tough, courageous private eye struggling to maintain his honor, dignity, and integrity without surrendering his style and refreshing wit. But he has grown significantly, especially in the area of self-knowledge, thanks in part to the frequent confrontations between his conscience and his actions, but more importantly because of his ever-deepening relationship with Susan. Even when she is absent, as she is for much of *The Judas Goat*, her presence is felt. Spenser tells her at the end of the book, "It's like I need to love you to come back whole from where I sometimes go." He realizes that his profession often leads him to places of death and suffering, and he knows that he will sometimes be tainted by bloodshed. But during a quick trip from Montreal to Boston for a conference with Dixon, he visits her house in Smithfield and, struck by the quiet peacefulness of the neighborhood, is reminded that human life continues at a normal, undramatic level even while he is risking his life in a world of violence and death. Susan becomes for him the means of transference from the wilderness of his world to the civilized stability of hers. Parker's handling of Spenser's relationship with Susan effectively disproves Chandler's assertion that the love story and the detective story cannot exist in the same book. Not only do they coexist in Parker's novels, the love story adds an element of tension by serving as a poignant reminder of the vast distance that separates the mean streets from the quiet ones.

With each novel Parker has exhibited growing independence from his predecessors, confidently developing his own themes, characters, and stylistic idiom. Although one can still detect similarities between Spenser and Philip Marlowe, Lew Archer, and even Rex Stout's Archie Goodwin, Parker has successfully managed to establish Spenser's own separate identity as a private detective. However, despite his innovative efforts, he has remained faithful to the conventions of the genre, so effectively laid down by his predecessors. He has thus earned for himself the right to be designated *the* legitimate heir to the Hammett-Chandler-Macdonald tradition, which, thanks to the efforts of writers like Parker, shows no sign of diminishing.

2

Roger L. Simon

Roger Lichtenberg Simon, the son of a doctor, was born in New York City on November 22, 1943. The family later moved to Scarsdale, New York, where Simon attended school. In 1960, he entered Dartmouth College, earning a B.A. degree in English in 1964. Immediately afterward, he entered Yale University, where he received a Master of Fine Arts degree in playwriting in 1967. While a graduate student, he wrote his first novel, *Heir*, which was published in 1968. After completing his studies at Yale, Simon moved to Los Angeles to devote full time to writing screenplays (for United Artists, Twentieth Century-Fox, and Warner Brothers) and a second novel, *The Mama Tass Manifesto*, published in 1970.

During this period he also began reading the detective novels of Dashiell Hammett, Raymond Chandler, and Ross Macdonald. When his former editor, who had moved to Straight Arrow Press (a subsidiary of *Rolling Stone* magazine), suggested he begin another book, Simon decided to write a contemporary detective novel. The result was *The Big Fix*, published in 1973, which introduced private detective Moses Wine. The novel appeared with the enthusiastic endorsement of Ross Macdonald who, in a quote featured prominently on the cover, called the novel "a landmark" and described Simon as "the most brilliant new writer of private detective fiction in years." Macdonald was not alone in his praise for *The Big Fix*: the novel received the Mystery Writers of America Special Award and the John Creasey Award from the Crime Writers of Great Britian as the best first crime novel of the year. In 1978, it attained even greater popularity with the release of a film version (for which Simon wrote the screenplay), with Richard Dreyfuss as Moses

Wine. *The Big Fix* was followed by *Wild Turkey* (1975), and
Peking Duck (1979).

Simon lives in Los Angeles with his wife, Dyann Asimow
Simon, a screenwriter whom he met while both were students at
Yale. Married since 1965, they have two children, Raphael, born in
1967, and Jesse, in 1972.

Contemporary writers of hard-boiled fiction are deeply indebted
to Hammett, Chandler, and Macdonald, and Simon is no exception.
He acknowledges admiration for Hammett's "wonderful prose,"
Chandler's sense of place (he is "perhaps the best American landscape writer there is," in Simon's judgment), and Macdonald's
craftsmanship. Of Macdonald, Simon says he is "the best craftsman
ever in American detective fiction." And yet, like many of his
predecessors, Simon admits that his interests extend beyond the
mystery genre. His favorite writer, for example, is Balzac, and he
especially admires his success in capturing life in Paris through the
years in *La Comédie Humaine*; he confesses a similar interest:
"What I would like to do in a small way with my detective novels is
to develop the way it is to live in our society through the years." He
also adds that "the thing that is most interesting to me about detective fiction is the hero himself and how to change him and how
he changes in time." Simon's eagerness to comment on social issues
derives in part from his political views: he avows that he perceives
society in Marxist terms, although he concedes, "I live a very
bourgeois lifestyle. I like money. In other words, I don't stand behind my beliefs, I only write them." This apparent contradiction
between politics and lifestyle introduces a theme that can be traced
through all his writing.

Simon's first novel, *Heir* (1969), is the story of Marcus Rottner,
wealthy grandson of a Jewish racketeer who amassed a fortune in
the thirties by questionable means and eventually died in prison
while serving a sentence for perjury. Rottner has just killed his girl
friend by injecting her (perhaps accidentally) with a fatal overdose
of heroin, and the novel, written in diary form, depicts his futile
attempts to dispose of her body. Her corpse comes to represent the
burden of guilt he cannot escape, guilt arising both from her death
and from the hollow sense of uselessness he feels at living off his
grandfather's tainted money. Eventually the dual pressures pre-

cipitate a breakdown. The police discover him with the body, and he is convicted of murder and sentenced to prison. Through Rottner's character, Simon depicts the corrupting effects of money (Rottner's name even suggests decay) and satirizes its ability to insulate one, as it has him, from the important issues of the day— his only interest in the escalating war in Viet Nam, for example, is the names of the leaders of North and South Viet Nam, which he uses in the solitaire ping-pong games he perpetually plays. In his psychological portrait of this affluent, tormented youth, Simon thus manages to incorporate some social and political satire.

His second novel, *The Mama Tass Manifesto* (1970), is more openly political in its message. Written in the form of memoirs of Tanya "Tass" Gesner, the novel reviews her radical past, beginning with her Scarsdale High School days and continuing through her years at Columbia University. She and her husband Morrie created an outrageous puppet drama which satirized the evils of the American political structure. The play, designed to "spring the dormant American consciousness to revolution," instead becomes a cultural phenomenon, moving from street theatre to commercial theatre and finally to the stage of Caligula's Palace Dome in Las Vegas. Tass and Morrie use their profits for revolutionary activities—they purchase a tanker (which they rename Potemkim II), and manage to blow up an oil installation in the Gulf of Mexico. However, the act proves futile, the bombing explained away as an accident. Meanwhile, their puppet drama becomes even more popular, and the Gesners become national celebrities. The conflict between the desire to remain ideologically pure and the allurement of material success is dramatized in the character of Morrie Gesner (like Simon, the son of a Scarsdale physician). While Tass successfully resists the temptations of success, Morrie succumbs and buys an expensive sports car. Eventually, however, consumed by guilt and frustration over selling out to the establishment, he walks into the path of a speeding car on an Oklahoma freeway and kills himself. The novel ends with Tass's hope that the future might bring a more receptive climate for social and political change in America.

Both *Heir* and *The Mama Tass Manifesto* develop themes that reappear in the Moses Wine novels: inequities in the social and political structure of American society; the conflict between ideology and material success; the compromises that threaten the commitment of the artist (or radical). In addition, several targets of Simon's satirical barbs—suburbia (Morrie Gesner is described as being "formed and deformed in the womb of Scarsdale, riddled with the confusion and disease of American society"); liberal-chic audiences that mindlessly applaud Tass's play while ignoring its political message; the comic excesses of the contemporary American cultural scene (Tass's puppet drama is eventually performed on the stage of Caligula's Pleasure Dome alongside seventy-five topless showgirls who form the peace symbol to the accompaniment of instrumental versions of Bob Dylan protest songs)—find their way into the detective novels. Artistically, the two novels also demonstrate Simon's skill in revealing character through first-person narration, an important technique in the writing of hard-boiled novels, most of which depend upon the effective creation of the narrator-hero's voice for their distinctive flavor.

When he began thinking about a third novel, Simon saw an opportunity to combine his political interests and concern for social issues with his admiration for the hard-boiled detective novels he had been reading, and so began writing *The Big Fix*. However, unlike Robert Parker, who was motivated at least initially by a desire to create another Philip Marlowe, Simon saw a chance to introduce a more contemporary private detective. Instead of simply continuing the tradition as it existed, he sought to modernize it, to update it in the light of the contemporary social, political, and cultural crosscurrents which had molded him.

THE BIG FIX

Attention, as well as tribute, ought to be paid to any writer courageous enough to attempt the difficult task of creating a new hard-boiled detective hero with any hope of developing a series around him. The hazards are many, the odds against success formidable. Readers expect the novels to follow certain conventions and the hero to bear a strong resemblance to his predecessors. But each writer has his own original ideas, his own unique talents, and so finds himself torn between the demands of imitation and the equally strong desire for innovation. Many hard-boiled series have died aborning either because their heroes were such pale imitations they were virtually indistinguishable from previous private detectives or were so unique as to be unrecognizable as belonging to the same genus as Sam Spade, Philip Marlowe, and Lew Archer. Only the most talented writers are able to solve the problem by striking an artful balance between imitation and innovation. Robert Parker is one example, Roger L. Simon another. But where Parker weights the balance on the side of imitation, Simon opts for innovation. A product of the political, moral, social, and sexual upheaval of the sixties, it is only natural that his creative imagination is fueled by different sources than many of his contemporaries, including Parker. And so although Simon's private detective, Moses Wine, is a professional colleague of Spade, Marlowe, and Archer, he is also plainly of a different generation.

It isn't simply in the conception of the hero where the differences are noticeable; in style, language, attitudes, even themes, Simon contributes something new, some contemporary slant. A writer of his generation who aims at recapturing the traditional hard-boiled atmosphere might easily be swayed by the temptation to parody the forties style. Simon avoids this by capturing the essence of the hero and retaining the conventions of the genre, then recreating and filtering both through his (and his generation's) cultural consciousness. The result is *The Big Fix* (1973), a novel which effectively updates the genre in contemporary terms without going as far, say, as Robert Altman who, in his film version of Raymond Chandler's *The Long Goodbye*, placed a forties-style Philip Marlowe in the Los Angeles of the seventies in order to show a hero whom the modern world has all but passed by. Simon's novel paints a vivid picture of modern Los Angeles, but his hero is very much at home in that city. Both the hero and the city have changed simultaneously. Simon remains true to the conventions of the genre, but he is also true to the spirit of his times and manages to combine both in a fresh reworking of the classic form of the hard-boiled novel.

What kind of man is Moses Wine? Tough. Cynical. Lonely.

Committed. All the qualities one usually associates with the traditional hard-boiled detective describe him. By character and disposition, he belongs to their fraternity. But as a man of his age (and, at thirty, several years younger than most of his colleagues), his character casts a more contemporary shadow. No bourbon and rumpled suits for him: his taste in clothing runs to denim, his hair is long, and he prefers dope to whiskey. Unlike Marlowe, Archer, and Spenser, each of whom took up private detective work following employment with the police, Wine is a law school dropout, an ex-Berkeley radical whose political views led him into the profession—when a lawyer friend needed help in proving a cop beat up a demonstrator, he took the case. The traditional private detective is invariably a man of the people, "the honest proletarian," in the words of Leslie Fiedler, "illuminating by contrast the decadent society of the rich." But where most of his fictional colleagues are motivated by an instinctive affinity for the common man, for the down and out, Wine acts more out of conviction, from a political philosophy. His Marxist views are closer to the surface than theirs. From his first protests against the House Un-American Activities Committee in 1960 through his active involvement in antiwar demonstrations at Berkeley, his actions have reflected his political views. Had he remained in law school, he might well have turned out to be "a nice young Jewish lawyer with a Matisse drawing on the office wall and twenty young draft dodgers as admirers," but he has rejected that role in favor of the kind of investigative work that has earned for him a reputation as "The People's Detective."

Wine, too, is cynical, but his cynicism is less indistinct than that experienced by many of his colleagues; in his case, it arises from disillusionment with the social and political realities of his time. As he explains in *Wild Turkey*, "It wasn't that I didn't have any faith in human nature. I still had some left, somewhere. It was just that the last decade of American life had reduced it to the size of a desiccated pea." Like his older colleagues, his cynicism only barely masks a romantic nostalgia, but where theirs usually emerges as a longing for the distant past, for a golden age of innocence that has been irretrievably lost, his takes the shape of memories of the good old days at Berkeley, the era of radical protest when he could flaunt his idealism against the forces of repression. Now that the protests have all ended, he has to struggle to preserve the remnants of that ideal-

ism in the face of changing political currents. Even his loneliness is
of a decidedly different hue, less a case of temperament than situation—he is divorced from his wife, Suzanne, and separated from his
sons, Jacob, four, and Simon, one, whom he sees only on Saturdays.

The Big Fix opens with Wine in his Los Angeles apartment
late one evening, smoking hash and playing solitaire *Clue*, trying
to decide whether Colonel Mustard or Mrs. Peacock committed the
murder. There is a knock at the door, and Wine opens it to find a
very attractive woman canvassing the neighborhood for Senator
Miles Hawthorne, a candidate for the Democratic presidential nomination in the upcoming California primary. Wine invites her in and,
as he answers her questions, suddenly recognizes her as Lila Shea,
a fellow Berkeley radical whom he has not seen in five years, not
since the night they made love in a 1952 Chrysler hearse parked
across the street from an antiwar protest at the Oakland Induction
Center. Lila has sought him out to obtain his assistance with a
serious problem that has arisen in Hawthorne's campaign. Hundreds
of flyers have appeared announcing support for Hawthorne by
Howard Eppis, radical leader of the Free Amerika Party, who has
suddenly emerged after years of living underground. Eppis promises
that Hawthorne "will do for Amerika what Mao and Lenin have
done for China and Russia." Hawthorne's supporters fear that Eppis's
endorsement will scare regular Democrats away from their candidate and with the election so close, even a small erosion of support
will result in the election of Governor Dillworthy, Hawthorne's
opponent. Lila wants Wine to find out what Eppis is up to and stop
him. Ordinarily Wine would have no interest in becoming involved
in what he cynically calls the "fetid stench of bigtime politics," but
because of his friendship with Lila, he agrees to help. He cares little
about the purity of the American electoral process and makes it
clear he is *not* a volunteer for Hawthorne; he insists on being paid
his fee, three hundred dollars a week.

He commences his search for Howard Eppis by visiting his last
known address, which turns out to be an abandoned Gothic mansion
in Venice, California. Inquiries to the editor of Eppis's book, *Rip It
Off* (Eppis appears to be an amalgam of such sixties radical leaders
as Jerry Rubin and Abbie Hoffman, author of a book entitled *Steal
This Book*), and the producer of a record he once made are equally
fruitless; neither has heard from Eppis in years. But Wine does

learn something interesting—the owner of the record company
which released Eppis's record, Oscar Procari, Jr., son of a wealthy
California financier, ended up with Eppis's girl friend. Her name was
Lila Shea. This lead proves to be a dead end when Wine learns that
Procari committed suicide two years earlier. However, he realizes
his investigation is producing results when he notices he is being
followed by two men in a car with Nevada license places. But before
he can make any sense out of this development, events take a sudden and tragic turn—Lila Shea is killed when her car goes over a
cliff less than a mile from Wine's apartment. A bottle of barbiturates
found in her car leads the police to conclude she died accidentally,
but Wine is too suspicious about the circumstances of her death to
believe it was anything but murder. Whatever hesitation he initially
had about working for a politician disappears now that he has a
compelling personal reason to continue the investigation.

He resumes his search for the mysterious Howard Eppis by
seeking out Alora Vazquez, a beautiful Mexican woman he met
earlier in a bar under suspicious circumstances—he thought she was
attempting to seduce him but discovered she was actually trying to
trick him into leaving the bar, for which she was hired, she confesses, by the two men in the car with Nevada plates Wine spots
parked outside. He finds her and follows her to a Mexican market
in East Los Angeles, where he is suddenly accosted by a group of
Mexican men who beat him up; only when he mentions the name of
Don Villarejo of the Barrio Defense League, who vouches for Wine
as the man responsible for saving a Chicano from a frame-up, is he
saved. Alora's friends were following him because they suspected he
had something to do with the mysterious disappearance of Luis
Vazquez, Alora's father. They were given the address of the same
abandoned mansion in Venice Wine was and became suspicious
when they saw him nosing around the place. Wine assures them he
had nothing to do with Vazquez's disappearance. They let him go,
but leave him with another mystery to solve—what, if anything,
does Luis Vazquez's disappearance have to do with Howard Eppis?

Things soon go from bad to worse. San Sebastian, Hawthorne's
Los Angeles Coordinator and Wine's employer, receives another
letter from Eppis, this one hinting at a possible bombing of the Los
Angeles freeway system in his campaign of "support" for Hawthorne.
As Wine and Sebastian drive around discussing what to do next,

they discover they are being followed by the omnipresent Nevada car. They escape, but not without being shot at. The next day, another surprise—Sebastian disappears, his office cleaned out. It now appears that he might have been a Dillworthy spy in the Hawthorne organization. Wine's troubles are multiplying rapidly: a friend is killed; he has been beaten up and shot at; his leads keep running into dead ends; new mysteries keep arising; his ex-wife wants more money; he worries about his kids; the police consider him a suspect in Lila Shea's death; and he hasn't had sex in three months. To top it all off, Howard Eppis is planning to blow up the freeways in a few days, and he is no closer to finding him than when he began.

Intrigued by how often the name Oscar Procari keeps popping up, especially when Procari's father invites him to his Rolling Hills estate to hire him to find his son (even though he apparently committed suicide two years earlier by driving his sports car over a cliff), Wine does some investigating into Procari's death. He locates the doctor who signed the death certificate (a shady character who now runs an abortion factory at the airport for the convenience of young girls flying in from out of state) and wrests an admission from him that he turned Procari's bones over to a man named Jonas, who paid him $5,000. The name strikes a bell. During the encounter with the men in the Nevada car who shot at him and Sebastian, he thought he heard Sebastian say to one of them, "Jonas, don't do it . . . please." Sebastian claimed Wine misunderstood, that he said, "Jesus, don't do it." Acting on a hunch that Jonas and the Nevada car might be related, Wine calls a friend in the Las Vegas defender's office and learns that a man named Phil Jonas is widely-known in Nevada for involvement in gambling and prostitution. He doesn't have much to go on, only the name of Jonas's hangout, the Palm Casino at Tonopah, but with time running out, it's the only lead he has, so he heads for Nevada.

Wine doesn't find Jonas, but his trail does lead him to the Cottonwood Meadows, a brothel in the middle of the Nevada desert where he meets a beautiful young prostitute. A wealthy rancher out for an adventure with his son notices Wine's interest in the girl and tells him it's his lucky day, he'll pay for the girl. Wine is sorely tempted to accept his offer, but he reminds himself he has a job to do. On the other hand, remembering that he hasn't had sex in three months, he argues, "It had been a long time. Besides, who cared about a murder and a big election fix? They could wait." First things first. A brief fling with the girl just might take his mind off his worries. This episode certainly appears to sound the death knell to the traditional image of the chaste and chivalric knight who places personal needs and desires aside in his single-minded pursuit of truth and justice. Even Spenser, for all his open-mindedness about sex, never let lust interfere with the performance of his duty. Wine is simply too contemporary for all that chivalric nonsense (and he isn't all that committed to Hawthorne in the first place). As far as he can see, a temporary delay can't hurt.

Simon doesn't go to all this trouble to get Wine into the Nevada brothel just to provide him with a pleasant sexual interlude. It turns out that Cottonwood Meadows also houses a large-scale gambling operation (where bets are placed on such things as the Florida Little League championship and the outcome of the civil war in Nigeria), and who should arrive unexpectedly but none other than Oscar Procari, Sr. The pieces begin to fall neatly into place now, especially after Wine is seized by Procari's men and finds himself locked up with Sam Sebastian, who admits he is in reality the supposedly dead Oscar Procari, Jr. He reveals that the body found in his car two years earlier actually belonged to Howard Eppis, who was murdered and whose bones provided "evidence" for his supposed suicide. Eppis's reemergence as a Hawthorne supporter was masterminded by the elder Procari, with the help of his weak, submissive son, in order to insure victory for Dillworthy. Procari and his gambling associates have bet ten million dollars on the California primary and intend to protect their investment by ruining Hawthorne. However, their plans are foiled when Wine escapes and drives a stolen motorcycle back to Los Angeles in time to prevent the explosion of the bomb, which was placed at the intersection of the Hollywood and Harbor freeways in downtown Los Angeles.

With the bombing averted, the loose ends can now be tied up. Acting on a hunch, Wine returns to the fake Norman castle of Isabel La Fontana, a celebrated local "witch" he first met in connection with his investigation into one of those strange California occult religions, "The Church of the Five Deities," founded by the younger Procari. Wine finds both Procaris there, confirming his suspicion that La Fontana is really Mrs. Procari. Procari, who takes him captive again, admits that Wine is right in many of his conclusions: Eppis was killed when he suspected that "The Church of the Five Deities" was only a front for his gambling operation; Lila Shea was murdered and Luis Vazquez kidnapped because both apparently suspected that Eppis was no longer alive, a disclosure which would ruin his plan. Now Procari must get rid of Wine. Suddenly shots ring out and Procari falls dead, fatally wounded by Luis Vazquez, who was being held prisoner in La Fontana's house. Young Procari, seeing an opportunity to stop his father, but unable to do it himself, freed Vazquez, who killed him. The big fix is stopped, the mysteries are all solved, and Hawthorne wins the primary election.

The plot of *The Big Fix* is intricate and involved, tightly woven with ingenious puzzles, cunning imposters, and all sorts of ruses and schemes. Simon manages to keep all the elements under control, manipulating the pace and unravelling the surprises at well-timed intervals. And there are more than enough mysteries to keep the reader interested: Where is Howard Eppis?; Who killed Lila Shea?; What does Luis Vazquez have to do with the case?; Why does Oscar Procari's name keep turning up?; Will Wine be able to preserve victory for Hawthorne? Everything is neatly resolved at the end, perhaps too neatly, a weakness often found in novels with such complicated plots. Loose ends protrude, nagging questions remain after all the dust has settled: Why was Lila Shea killed and not Luis Vazquez?; What purpose does the Vazquez subplot serve? Or the occult subplot with Isabel La Fontana? Why would Oscar Procari encourage Wine's suspicions by hiring him to find his son, whom he knows is alive and whose discovery would undermine his plan? In retrospect, such questions expose Simon's plot weaknesses, although they do not detract from the exciting flow of the narrative toward its dramatic conclusion.

Centering the plot on a political campaign enables Simon to reveal some of Wine's basic attitudes while at the same time permitting him to introduce his own views about the political situation in America. Simon is, at best, distrustful of the American electoral system, and Wine's comments obviously reflect his views. For example, Wine's description of Governor Dillworthy is a satiric caricature of the grovelling, unscrupulous politician whose unbridled ambition has brought him to within a hair's breadth of the Democratic nomination for President of the United States:

Dillworthy was something else again. His face was pancaked in layers, his hair lacquered and retouched follicle by follicle. He must have spent more hours in make-up than Gloria Swanson before she descended the staircase. He looked like an interior decorator from a smallish Midwestern city whose clients were beginning to desert him. He wanted to win so badly he was constantly on the brink of tears, as if the threat of an imminent emotional collapse in front of millions of people would convince them to vote for him out of a sense of propriety. Don't let it come to this, folks. Don't have my public breakdown on your shoulders . . . And when he wasn't whining, he was flailing about in righteous indignation, berating Hawthorne for anything his little mind could think of. He would have accused him of pederasty under the bleachers of Dodger Stadium, if he could have gotten away with it.

On the other hand, Wine's view of Miles Hawthorne is more measured, thus revealing an important ambivalence in his attitude. He has little trouble rejecting Hawthorne as a typical politician, yet he cannot ignore his worth as an individual, and the tension between the two views makes him uneasy. For example, he is forced to conclude that Hawthorne is a decent man but confesses, "I didn't want to recognize that at first. It was too much of a shock to see it in a politican, an aberration of the human personality too extreme to trust—like meeting a bookie with a social conscience—but it was there all the same." Even though Hawthorne supports several proposals with which he agrees—decriminalization of grass, guaranteed minimum income, national health insurance—Wine cannot avoid the cynical conclusion that, after all, he is only "a Democratic politican at campaign time." As election day approaches and he finds himself actually rooting for Hawthorne, he admits, "I wasn't sure I liked myself for it. Once you began to place your trust in a politician you were something of a fool. You ran the risk he would betray you for the next vote. And he surely would."

Whenever Wine's political conscience wavers, his radical Aunt Sonya is there to keep him ideologically pure. Sonya is a feisty old woman who as a youth fought the Czar's dragoons on the steps of the Winter Palace and later escaped a Stalinist labor camp; now, in her midseventies, she knits afghans with portraits of Trotsky in the middle, but she has lost nothing of that old radical fire. She is, if anything, even more cynical about politics than her nephew. When Dillworthy visits the Fairfax Senior Citizens Center where she lives and makes the mistake of asking how she likes living there, she lets him have it, telling him it's a "shit-hole." When he embarrassedly promises to look into the situation, she says, "my ass you will; one of your biggest backers owns the place." When Wine informs Sonya he is working for Hawthorne, she is aghast: "Better you should tell me your youngest son is having a lobotomy." She even strives to inculcate Wine's four-year-old son Jacob with the proper political attitudes; when Wine mentions he is going to watch election night coverage on television, Jacob reminds him that, according to Aunt Sonya, "elections are the opium of decadent democracy." (In *Peking Duck*, Wine reveals that Sonya even tried unsuccessfully to teach him the words to "The Internationale" in Russian when he was seven.)

Despite such vocal bulwarks to his political conscience, Wine remains ambivalent, an attitude which humanizes him by sparing him from an overly self-righteous posture. His uncertainty dramatizes his situation as a thirty-year-old man whose radical past is unmistakably behind him and who must now make certain adjustments to society (as Lila Shea did by becoming involved in Hawthorne's campaign). Whether he likes it or not, he must operate in a society whose values are frequently at odds with his. Furthermore, he has family obligations, middle-class responsibilities, and must find suitable means of providing for his sons. He has dropped out of law school because he could not see himself in the role of prosperous attorney, but he is still searching to determine the extent to which he must accomodate himself to society, to see how long he can remain "the last hold-out for alienation in a world of engaged men." Like many of his fictional colleagues, Wine is an anachronism, but whereas Marlowe, Archer, and Spenser, among others, are anachronistic by virtue of their roles as knights defending old-fashioned virtues against the corruption of the modern world, Wine's anachronism emerges from his displacement as a sixties radical in the peaceful (and apathetic) seventies.

Wine's commitment to social issues runs deep, and he prides himself at spurning certain materialistic values; he rejects, for example, the life-style represented by his former law school colleagues who, he predicts, will in twenty years be "just like my New York relatives, riding through Harlem in their late-model Lincoln limousines with the windows rolled up for the air conditioning and the radio tuned to WBAI." His description of a photograph of Luis Vazquez, with "one of those fine weathered Mexican faces that proved you could learn more from a year in the fields than ten in the library," discloses his proletarian sympathies. But an important distinction can be made here between Wine and Spenser. Spenser is often accused by characters he meets of having a social worker's conscience because of the concern he exhibits for the welfare of his clients. This is not quite the same as being attracted, as Wine is, to clients because they represent a certain social class. Spenser's and Wine's attitudes are similar, but their motivations differ.

A comparison of the film version of *The Big Fix* (which Simon wrote) with the novel reveals some significant alterations in theme. The character of Wine remains essentially intact, but there are numerous plot changes (the entire Nevada episode, the occult subplot, and the character of Isabel La Fontana, among other things, are all eliminated), the effect of which is to simplify the action, thus placing more emphasis on the political theme. It is here where the changes are most noticeable. For one thing, the political and moral distinctions between Dillworthy and Hawthorne are eradicated. In the novel, Wine was forced to recognize Hawthorne's basic decency, even to agree with many of his positions; in the film, Hawthorne is shown to be as incompetent as Dillworthy. (He is said to have changed his position on capital punishment four times in three years.) Also, the motive for the fix is changed from greed to politics, and the election is shifted from a presidential primary to a California gubernatorial election, with Procari and his friends transformed into right-wingers who aim to insure the election of Dillworthy to protect their political interests. The result of such changes is to magnify the political cynicism of the book. The movie proposes that all politicians are inept, that there is little to choose between them, and that special interest groups have no hesitation in fixing elections for the benefit of their own candidate. The film, with its heightened emphasis on political dirty tricks, also allows Simon to update his theme in light of the Watergate scandals which occurred after the publication of the novel.

One other important change in the film serves to make more

explicit a theme that is only implied in the novel. In the film, Howard Eppis turns up alive at the end, living in a comfortable suburban home, enjoying a successful new career in advertising. He tells Wine that he has simply transferred his sloganeering skills to the writing of commercials. After all, he explains, they require the same talents; besides, he confesses, it's difficult to remain a radical in this country, hard to say no to all the goodies. (The enticement to compromise one's principles at Mammon's call is also an important theme in Simon's *The Mama Tass Manifesto*.) Eppis's resurrection in the film serves no plot function; its real purpose is to illustrate Simon's view concerning the temptation to sell out. In the book, when Wine sees a poster announcing Eppis's support for Hawthorne, he notes sadly that "the dreams of one decade [are] degraded by the next." This theme is developed more explicitly in the film, not only through the character of Eppis but also in such scenes as Wine's visit to a radical law school professor's class, where the students are shown to be interested only in grades, no longer in issues. Even his source of information is altered to reflect this theme: he extracts material from a lawyer friend by threatening to expose his radical past, which he is attempting to keep hidden so as not to jeopardize his political future. Wine's sentimental attitude toward the good old days surfaces in the film when, as he views newsreel footage of a sixties antiwar march, he begins to weep, recognizing that the activism and idealism of the sixties have given way to the pragmatism and narcissism of the seventies. Changes such as these only underscore the suspicion that Simon's primary interest in the detective genre is in its effectiveness as a vehicle for commentary on contemporary American life. In this he is no different from writers such as Chandler, Macdonald, and Parker, only more openly political in his orientation.

Like all private detectives, Wine finds himself in an adversary relationship with the police, but in his case it arises less from professional differences than political ones. To him, the police represent the establishment, the enemy he remembers from his Berkeley days when they were the "pigs" bent on repressing all forms of dissent. They are also to be denounced for their unwarranted violation of citizens' rights, for their blatant invasion of privacy. (Wine discovers that his whole past is a matter of police record, including a photograph of him with Lila Shea taken years earlier.) For their part, the police, represented in the novel by Detective Sergeant Koontz, distrust Wine not simply because he is a private detective; he is suspect because of his leftist politics. Koontz calls Wine "Chairman Mao's favorite private eye," and when he arrives at his apartment to question him about Lila Shea's death, he remarks with feigned surprise, "What're you doing here? The last plane for Peking left an hour ago," a jab at his radical politics (and a prophetic remark, since Wine actually does go to Peking in his third case, *Peking Duck*). Additionally, Wine has to endure ethnic as well as political slurs, with Koontz variously referring to him as Weinberg, Wiener, or Weinstein. Most private detectives are distrusted by the police because of their independence or their integrity. Wine is hated because he is a Jewish peacenik.

Like most of his fictional colleagues, Wine leads a lonely life, but in his case the loneliness is less the result of chronic malaise than the recent failure of his marriage. He has been separated from his wife, Suzanne, for almost a year. Now his life is complicated by her constant demands for money (which he doesn't have; he cannot even deposit the three hundred dollars he earns in the Hawthorne case for fear his creditors will attach his bank account), his concern for his two sons (of whom he has custody on Saturdays), and a lingering sexual jealousy. He has been celibate for three months (not apparently by choice) and still winces with jealousy each time he finds Suzanne with her latest lover, a guru named Madas. Despite their separation, caused largely by her disappointment with his choice of detective work over a more promising legal career, he finds himself still attracted to her. During one visit, he catches himself staring wistfully at "her good breasts coming through the cotton" of her flimsy gown. On another occasion, after a frustrating failure to seduce Alora Vazquez, he finds himself heading for Suzanne's house, apparently with the hope of making love with her. When he arrives, however, he discovers her already making love with Madas and quietly leaves to return home and masturbate. His sexual funk is created by the frustrations involving the women in his life: his wife is unavailable; Alora Vazquez is uninterested; Lila Shea is dead. Hence, his encounter with the prostitute at the Cottonwood Meadows is only a brief oasis of pleasure in the celibate life he is trying so hard to overcome.

Alienation from his wife is only one cause of his domestic

agony; separation from his sons is another. Living three freeways away, seeing them only on weekends, he worries whether he is being a good father to them. Thus, the Procari father-son relationship holds a special importance for him. The destructive effect of the dominant, overbearing father on the passive son who suppresses his own wishes and principles because he is too weak to oppose the father, until he can finally summon enough courage to rise up against him (even though he cannot actually pull the trigger that kills him), reminds us of the Oedipal material that characterizes Ross Macdonald's novels. But unlike Archer, a father-surrogate whose investigations into other people's lives often become symbolic searches for a son (the son he never had, the son he once was), Wine has two very real sons and his investigations are characterized not by any symbolic search for the son but instead by the very real search for a babysitter. (Maintaining an effective surveillance while worrying about your kids is one problem his colleagues never had to face.) The Procari subplot provides the kind of mirroring relationship Parker uses so effectively in his novels. Wine's involvement with the Procaris induces a real concern for his sons' future, and the novel ends on this note: "Being a father was a tough gig. I wondered if in some unconscious way I was warping my sons as surely as Procari had. I hoped not." Although the political aspects of the case do not touch him personally, the Procari relationship does. Wine thus emerges as a man whose success in solving the case is of secondary importance to his concern for success as a father.

When his various problems—his family worries, his sexual frustration, his stalled investigation, his loneliness—become too oppressive, Wine turns to the only sources of escape available to him: he either plays solitaire *Clue* (an echo of Marlowe's fascination with chess problems) or smokes dope. While his more traditional colleagues stick to alcohol, Wine, a product of the sixties, is drawn more to the anesthetizing qualities of the weed. He occasionally worries that he might be befogging his brain by smoking too much dope, but is relieved when he remembers that Sherlock Holmes took three cocaine injections daily and lay upon his sofa for days on end hardly speaking or moving. Satisfied that he is still far from this stage, he relaxes and enjoys the assuaging effects of the hash.

Although *The Big Fix* is Simon's third novel, it represents his initial attempt at writing in the mystery genre, and it reveals certain weaknesses: the plot, for example, raises some unanswered questions and certain incidents strain credulity; several characters are sketchily drawn; the portrait of young Procari is not as psychologically convincing as it might be; and his relationship with his father is not adequately dramatized. On the other hand, the action is fast-paced and exciting; the character of Wine is interesting and shows enormous potential for development; Simon's style, although lacking the color of Chandler's, the poetic beauty of Macdonald's, and the wit of Parker's, nevertheless is fresh and speaks in a contemporary voice. (Wine's description of Eppis's prose in *Rip It Off* as sounding "like a bad underground disc jockey on uppers" employs a simile that is characteristic of the sixties.) Simon's picture of Los Angeles is equally contemporary. Marlowe and Archer would have no trouble recognizing such locations as the deserted Gothic mansion in Venice or Oscar Procari's Rolling Hills estate nor such characters as the unscrupulous doctor, incompetent police, and religious charlatans that populate Simon's novel. But the recording studio at Grit Records, with its spaced-out musicians and speed-freak, suede-suited publicity director, and Hawthorne's political headquarters, with its computer print-outs and media conscious advisors, give the picture a more contemporary hue. Simon's sense of place is excellent, and as Wine ranges from colorful El Mercado, the Mexican market in East Los Angeles, to the Jewish neighborhood on Fairfax Avenue, and from the manicured Procari estate in Rolling Hills to the seedy decadence of Venice, the novel presents a crazy quilt view of the city that has become synonymous with the American private eye.

Like Parker's *The Godwulf Manuscript, The Big Fix* represents an auspicious debut, a most promising introduction to a series. A brief comparison between both novels, however, reveals an essential difference in their respective authors' intentions. Parker's interest is in continuing the tradition; in the Spenser novels, he introduces several original features and writes in his own unique style, yet he always stays within the context of the hard-boiled tradition. When he imitates a standard scene or borrows a convention from a classic detective novel (as he does often in *The Godwulf Manuscript*), it is always done in homage. Simon is interested in something a little different. When he draws attention to a convention, it is usually to emphasize the difference between past and present. Wine is also a more accurate reflection of his time than Spenser is, and so where one could imagine Spenser in Marlowe's world, one cannot picture Wine in that world or Marlowe in Wine's. Simon deftly refashions the genre enough to accomodate the character of his very contemporary hero, thus proving convincingly that you *can* put new Wine in old bottles.

WILD TURKEY

Six months have passed since Moses Wine saved the primary election for Miles Hawthorne and his life has undergone some changes. He has had to replace his battered '47 Buick (a casualty of his desert encounter with Oscar Procari) with a '65 Jag XKE and has cut his hair and exchanged his denim for slacks and a blazer. ("I was finding it difficult to investigate bank presidents in a tie-dye tee shirt and jeans.") His domestic situation is as unsettled as ever: his wife is off somewhere in Europe "finding herself," so he has custody of his two sons, the younger of whom is still not completely toilet-trained. He loves the boys but finds their presence something of a hindrance in the free and unrestricted pursuit of his profession. His life is further disrupted by the dramatic arrival of Dr. Gunther Thomas, famous writer, culture hero, and "Ph.D. in guerilla journalism" (and dead ringer for the originator of Gonzo journalism, *Rolling Stone* writer Hunter S. Thompson), who climbs through his bedroom window at 5 A.M. one morning and announces he is going to do a feature on the "stoned Sam Spade" for *Rolling Stone*. He tells Wine to wait, he'll be right back with a photographer.

Thirteen months later, he returns with the photographer and a case for Wine: Deborah Frank, anchorwoman on the ABC Morning News, has been found murdered in her suite at the Beverly Wilshire Hotel, and the prime suspect is noted author Jock Hecht (a Norman Mailer-like character whose career, like Mailer's, was launched twenty-five years earlier with a novel about World War II). Wine is hesitant, having promised his son Jacob that he would take him to the museum. But when Jacob's friend invites him to go fishing instead, Wine is free to accompany Thomas to the Chateau Marmont, where Hecht is living. With two-and-a-half-year-old Simon in hand, Wine and Thomas arrive at Hecht's apartment and are greeted by the sound of his voice and the ecstatic moans and squeals of some women inside. Thomas barges in, interrupting Hecht and a pair of attractive coeds in the midst of "research" for his book, *Sex in America: One Man's Journey*. Hecht admits he is not particularly interested in Wine's help, but is being pressured by his publishers to hire a private detective to clear his name. Hecht unfortunately has a good motive for murdering Deborah Frank— they were widely known antagonists, she branding him publicly as a fraud, poseur, and impotent drunk, he accusing her of being a sexual reactionary—but he also claims to have a good alibi: at the time of her murder, he tells Wine, he was wrestling with a nude girl named Meiko at the Kama Sutra Sexual Phrontistery on Santa Monica Boulevard. (Alibis have certainly become more interesting since the days of Philip Marlowe.) Wine finds a babysitter for Simon (Alora Vazquez, the beautiful Mexican woman from *The Big Fix*, with whom he has been having an affair) and heads for the Sexual Phrontistery to talk with Meiko. Posing as a customer, he tells the receptionist he is interested in sampling this sensational Oriental girl a friend has recommended he try. The girl smiles knowingly and says, "Now I understand . . . You're a friend of Jock Hecht! He calls all the girls Meiko!"

Realizing that Hecht's alibi is worthless, and furious at him for concocting such a ridiculous story, Wine returns to the Chateau Marmont to confront him, only to discover his body in the bathroom, a bullet in his head. In his typewriter, he finds a note in which Hecht admits killing Deborah Frank. With her murder apparently solved and with Hecht now dead, Wine's investigation comes to an abrupt halt. But the unexpected arrival of Hecht's beautiful red-haired, green-eyed wife Nancy, an English professor at Hunter College in New York, changes things. Convinced that her husband was too egotistical to commit suicide, she hires Wine to find his murderer and gives him the name of a prime candidate—gangster Meyer Greenglass, currently serving a prison term for credit card fraud.

Nancy claims Greenglass blames his conviction on Hecht because he was indicted only a week after Hecht concluded his research on him for a book on the Jewish mafia. Wine agrees to help and drives to the Terminal Island prison to question Greenglass, who denies having anything to do with Hecht's death.

The only other lead Wine has is a reference he finds in one of Hecht's journals to a Cindy at Topanga, "the first truly liberated person," so he decides to try and locate her. He has little trouble, for everybody in Topanga Canyon apparently knows Cindy, or Dr. Cynthia Hardwick, "noted sexual surrogate." (No doubt a pun is intended on the name Hardwick, which hints at the aim of her celebrated treatment for impotence.) At her house Wine is greeted by Cindy herself, an attractive fifty-year-old woman in a bikini who, assuming he has come for help, doffs the bikini and orders him to undress. Wine complies and before he knows it finds himself being sensuously massaged by Cindy, who quickly discovers that impotence is not Wine's problem. Undaunted, she suggests they not waste his erection. However, Gunther Thomas makes another of his dramatic entrances, reminds the "Dick Tracy of the streakers" that they have work to do, and saves (or deprives) Wine from an erotic adventure with Cindy. As they drive away, they are accosted by several Cubans who dump Thomas and take Wine to his apartment, where his sons are being held captive by the leader of the group, a man named Santiago Martin, who demands that Wine turn over the tapes he took from Hecht's office. Wine knows nothing about any tapes, but Martin warns him if he doesn't produce them in forty-eight hours, his sons will suffer the consequences. Martin has located Wine's most vulnerable spot, his children, and although he has no idea what Martin is talking about, or how the tapes might be connected to Hecht's death, he has just been given a compelling reason to find them.

Gunther Thomas comes to the rescue again. He introduces Wine to Sal Gruskow, a film producer who confirms that there really is a Meiko, that she has a bit part in a film he is making, and that she still works at the Kama Sutra Sexual Phrontistery. Wine returns to the Sexual Phrontistery just in time to see "the biggest goddamn vice raid I had ever seen, an incredible piece of over-kill, like using the entire Chinese Army to capture South Pasadena." He counts five prowl cars, an antiriot crew, two television crews, a member of

the Board of Supervisors, the City Attorney, his old nemesis Detective Koontz and, leading the whole operation, Frank Dichter,
Attorney General of the State of California, who announces to the
television cameras that "the trouble with this state is that we've
turned soft on sex." The closing of the Sexual Phrontistery is but the
first step in his all-out effort to rid the city of such establishments
(and the first step in his undeclared candidacy for the governorship
of California). The raid proves to be a real benefit to Wine too, for
when the Sexual Phrontistery's signs are removed, the identity of the
former occupant of the building is disclosed—a travel agency op-
erated by the same Santiago Martin who is threatening his kids.

Still frustrated in his attempts to find Meiko, Wine returns to
Gruskow for help only to learn that he too is having trouble finding
her, that she failed to show up to film her scheduled scenes. But he
does learn something helpful from Gruskow—the murdered Deborah Frank was in fact the *niece* of Meyer Greenglass. Supplied now
with an even better motive for Greenglass to have had Hecht murdered, Wine returns to the Terminal Island prison, but this time
Greenglass refuses to see him. However, Greenglass later sends a
message directing him to an announcement in *Variety* about the
shutting down of Gruskow's film because of a failure in the air
conditioning system. Wine, puzzled, visits the movie set and, nosing
around, discovers the reason for the air conditioning failure—he
locates Meiko's body stuffed in a duct above the set.

The mysteries abound. Who killed Meiko? How did Greenglass
know where her body was stashed unless he had her killed? But
what motive could he have for killing her? Did Hecht really commit
suicide, or did Greenglass have him killed because he murdered
his niece? What is the relationship between Santiago Martin and
the Sexual Phrontistery? What do the missing tapes have to do with
all of this? One of the mysteries is solved when Cindy Hardwick
reveals that the Sexual Freedom League, which owns the Liberation
Institute which she directs as well as half the sex clubs in Los
Angeles, is run by a group of Cubans led by Santiago Martin. The
tape mystery is clarified when Gunther Thomas discovers some old
newspaper clippings about the tenth anniversary of the aborted
Bay of Pigs invasion of Cuba. One of the photographs shows eight
members of the Third Battalion reunited for an anniversary cele-
bration. Wine recognizes two of the faces: Santiago Martin and his

battalion chief, Frank Dichter, now the Attorney General of California. Wine has found the missing link: Dichter is a silent partner
in the Sexual Freedom League with his former Cuban associates.
Wine concludes that the missing tapes probably contain incriminating evidence linking Dichter to the very same sex shops he is making
such a big issue out of closing down. Wine assumes that the murders
of Deborah Frank, Jock Hecht, and Meiko are related to Dichter's
attempts to obtain the tapes for himself in order to prevent disclosure of his involvement in the pornography business. Further
snooping ascertains that Dichter is innocent of murder, but proves
he is guilty of such things as extortion, hypocrisy, and corruption,
political evils Simon exposed in *The Big Fix*. As in that book,
politicians in *Wild Turkey* are depicted as unscrupulous types who
will do or say anything to get elected. If it is to Dichter's advantage
to institute a public campaign against sex, so be it, even if he is
forced to close the sex shops in which he has a financial interest.
One of the conventions of crime fiction, especially in the hard-boiled
novel, is the intimate link often existing between crime and respectability. Simon's variation on the convention is to place the
theme in a political context. In this post-Watergate age, he has
located it fittingly.

Proof of Dichter's secret partnership in the Sexual Freedom
League is obtained thanks to the dead Jock Hecht who, before
killing himself (which Wine concludes he did), sent Wine an advertisement for the House of Dominance in Redondo Beach with a
message scrawled in lipstick: "See Dolores—she delivers!" Wine
arranges a rendezvous of all the interested parties at the House of
Dominance, which quickly erupts into a bloody shootout between
Santiago Martin and his men and Dichter's man, who has been
following Wine. All but Wine are killed. When Detective Koontz
finally arrives, he and Wine search the house and find the tapes,
hidden under a dish belonging to Dolores, the cat. What Wine hears
on the tapes "made John Ehrlichman seem like St. Francis of
Assisi," but cynically he adds, "With any luck he [Dichter] would
get a heavy reprimand for this and lose his license to practice law in
San Bernardino." His distrust also extends to the police, so to insure
against Koontz or any "secretary" erasing the evidence, he phones a
reporter with the damaging revelations about Dichter.

Despite solution of the tape mystery, the murder of Deborah

Frank remains unsolved until Meyer Greenglass again provides a needed clue—he gives Wine a New York phone number. Wine calls the number and finds himself speaking with Bathsheba Hecht, Jock and Nancy's young daughter, who confesses she has missed her mother ever since her departure for California the previous Friday, the day *before* Nancy told Wine she had arrived, the day Deborah Frank was murdered. Suddenly (as is often the case in hard-boiled novels), suspicion falls upon the woman with whom the detective has fallen in love. Wine rushes to the airport in time to prevent Nancy from returning to New York and confronts her with his suspicions. She breaks down and confesses she murdered Deborah Frank, and describes the scene to Wine: when she arrived at Deborah's apartment, Jock wasn't there, but Deborah announced that she and Jock had fallen in love (their public feud was a charade designed to conceal their real relationship) and were about to go off together. When Jock arrived, he greeted his wife with a kiss and then began to fondle Deborah. The two tried to get Nancy to participate in a *ménage à trois*, but she refused. When Jock and Deborah proceeded to make love in front of her, she became enraged and, grabbing a knife, stabbed Deborah to death. She tells Wine she hired him out of guilt over her husband's death, hoping he could prove that she wasn't the cause of his suicide. Wine is faced with the painful decision of what to do with the woman he has been sleeping with for the past several days. His dilemma is compounded by his sympathy for her agony at confronting the humiliating reality of her husband's sexually liberated life-style. He is uncertain whether her violent response was crazy or only a "near-normal reaction" to the scene before her. He first considers, then rejects, the idea of fleeing the country with her, deciding instead to arrange for a former law school colleague to defend her on the murder charge. As he and Nancy leave her apartment the next morning to surrender to the police, a shot suddenly rings out and Nancy falls, "a wild turkey shot dead at four hundred yards."

Wine returns for a final visit with Meyer Greenglass, who admits that he ordered Nancy's death. He reveals that Deborah Frank was not his niece but his daughter, raised by his brother-in-law. It turns out that Wine has simply been acting as a pawn in Greenglass's hands, someone who could confirm the identity of his daughter's killer for him. Since Greenglass knew that Deborah and

Hecht were in love, he concluded Hecht did not kill her. Wine did
the footwork confirming his suspicions about Nancy Hecht and,
dying now of cancer and unwilling to turn her fate over to the
courts, he invoked the Mosaic law of an eye for an eye and ordered
her executed. He also solves Meiko's murder for Wine, explaining
that the only one who could have known that Hecht had the tapes
Martin wanted was the person who had taken them from the Sexual
Phrontistery to give them to Hecht. Her death proved it was she.
Meiko was killed by the Cubans who were out to regain the tapes in
order to use the incriminating evidence against Dichter recorded on
them to prevent him from closing down their sex establishments.
Like Philip Marlowe at the end of *The Long Goodbye*, Wine suf-
fers the embarrassment of realizing that he has been used, been
played for a fool. He has solved Deborah Frank's murder but only at
Greenglass's direction. And he has lost Nancy. Only the interven-
tion of Gunther Thomas a few days later saves the novel from the
note of despair that concludes *The Long Goodbye*. Returning to
Topanga Canyon to retrieve his car, Wine spots Gunther, Cynthia
Hardwick, and a group of nude revellers dancing along a ridge.
Thomas calls him over and announces that he has abandoned plans
for the *Rolling Stone* piece on him in favor of writing a script for
Sal Gruskow's new movie about a big-time politician who murders
a Chicano who is attempting to expose his involvement in the operation of some sex parlors. He tells Wine to cheer up and offers him
some wine. Soon the warmth of the sun and the effects of the wine
and dancing dissipate his depression, and the novel ends with Wine
shedding his clothes (once more) to join the happy revellers.

The plot of *Wild Turkey* is a marvel of inventiveness and
calculated surprise, without the annoying loose ends and questionable character motivation that marred *The Big Fix*. The unravelling
of the plot is handled skillfully, the surprises are well-timed. Two
of the most dramatic of these—the disclosure of Nancy Hecht's
guilt and the revelation of Meyer Greenglass's shrewd manipulation
of Wine—provide more than simple dramatic impact. Each forces
Wine to self-examination, either involving his own sexual attitudes
(would he have acted with the same insane sexual jealousy as
Nancy?) or his professional pride (how could he have been used
so effectively and so unwittingly by Greenglass?). In his handling of
plot, Simon exhibits greater skill than either Chandler or Parker,

both of whom place more emphasis on character and style. He more
closely resembles Ross Macdonald, especially in his deft handling
of a complicated plot, and Dashiell Hammett, with whose *Maltese
Falcon*, with its many surprises, double crosses, pursuit of a valuable
object, manipulation of character, and love interest involving the
woman who is eventually exposed as the killer, *Wild Turkey* has
much in common.

Sex dominates *Wild Turkey* the way politics did *The Big Fix*,
although not in any prurient sense. (Wine's encounter with the
prostitute in *The Big Fix*, for example, is more sexually explicit than
anything in *Wild Turkey*.) Simon's interest in sex is manifold; he
uses it to present a picture of liberated life-styles in the seventies,
to symbolize the restless search for identity and self-fulfillment, to
reveal attitudes toward a variety of related issues, such as censorship
and individual liberty, and finally as an object of satire.

The novel depicts a society in the full flowering of the sexual
revolution, a world (or at least a city) where every sexual need can
be satisfied, every fantasy fulfilled. From the Kama Sutra Sexual
Phrontistery on Santa Monica Boulevard (located right around the
corner from *The Devil in Miss Jones* and The Institute of Oral
Love), which specializes in hot body shampoos, nude counseling,
waterbed therapy, and nude wrestling, to the more "respectable"
Sexual Freedom Institute in Topanga Canyon, Simon portrays a
society in breathless, narcissistic pursuit of "liberation." Open sex
becomes simply a more visible manifestation of the same pursuit of
self that Wine's ex-wife Suzanne is engaged in. (In *The Big Fix*, she
was into meditation with her guru; in *Wild Turkey*, she is off on the
Island of Corfu pursuing hydroponics.) No one seems to have the
slightest interest any longer in politics, in social issues, in righting
society's wrongs. Simon's satirical attitude toward this whole movement can be detected in the following description of the Liberation
Institute:

> The Liberation Institute was marked by a large wooden placard
> over a chain link fence. The driveway was wider than the main
> road itself and led past a swimming pool, tennis courts, what
> appeared to be guest houses and through an expansive lawn to
> the main building at the top. This was an imposing edifice built
> in an improbable Tyrolean style with dark shingles and a canti-

levered overhanging roof. The surrounding grounds had been
elaborately landscaped with azaleas and delphiniums and me-
ticulously-clipped hedges. The whole place reminded me of a
Swiss sanitiarium for the wealthy disturbed.

We drove around the side to the parking lot and got out. It
was filled with expensive cars—Mercedes, Lincolns, Cadillacs
and Maseratis. The walkways were paved with marble and the
front door was made of bronze with a frieze of a naked couple
in the missionary position. You had to be pretty well-heeled to
take your liberation in a place like this. We rang the bell and a
peephole appeared in the left breast of the woman on the door.

The Institute, presided over by Cynthia Hardwick (who greets
callers with the inane message, "Good morning . . . and may this be
the first day of the rest of your life!"), is a Fantasyland for adults,
a place where people "leave behind civilization and its discontents
to rediscover their natural selves." When Wine and Nancy enter the
Institute, they are asked to remove their clothes. ("House rules.")
As they walk through the building, Wine sees a group of people
"discovering their natural selves" by fondling each other on a
Persian rug in front of a roaring fire. The sound of a gong from
another room signals Tantric yoga, where "the participants sit on
the floor in the lotus position staring into each other's eyes and
feeding each other sweetmeats until they are overcome with the
desire to make love." Such activities expose the absurdities of the
human potential movement which, in this case, equates the narcissistic pursuit of sexual gratification with liberation of the human
spirit.

Although he satirizes some of the more outrageous examples of
the new sexual freedom, Simon certainly does not endorse Dichter's
repressive campaign against pornography. At his press conference
during the highly publicized closing of the Kama Sutra Sexual
Phrontistery, Dichter charges that such "obvious prostitution masquerading as physical therapy" corrupts the minds of children and
weakens the public will. But when a reporter raises a question about
the danger in drawing such a fine line between the closing down of
these establishments and the repression of individual rights, Dichter
brushes the comment aside, promising that a committee in his office
will issue a report. The sexual revolution was fought over the
question of individual rights; with this Simon has no complaint. His

satire is aimed at the selfish pursuit of sexual pleasure in the name
of liberation, the intellectualizing that often accompanies it (calling
a massage parlor a phrontistery exemplifies this), and the tawdri-
ness and degeneration that ensues (illustrated by a sign above the
door of the Kama Sutra Sexual Phrontistery which features an ugly
Day-Glo painting of Botticelli's *The Birth of Venus*). When these
things happen, sexual freedom earns as much right to be satirized
as those politicians who publicly oppose it for personal and political advantage. Hypocrisy is where you find it. Like most of his
fictional colleagues, Wine reveals a streak of moralism, which can be
detected in his disgust at some of the more outrageous displays of
the new sexual freedom:

> I got into the car and drove home along Hollywood Boulevard,
> staring out at the passing parade of the nighttime city. It was a
> depressing sight. Even in the rain, the streets were lined with
> leathery whores and fourteen-year-old transvestites, six-foot
> black glitter queens in torn, gold stockings and feather boas.
> The whole society had gone decadent, but without style—a
> Weimar Republic with no cabarets and no George Grosz to
> draw it.

Thirty-five years earlier in *The Big Sleep*, Raymond Chandler located Arthur Geiger's pornographic bookstore on Hollywood Boulevard, only in those days it had to masquerade as a rare bookshop.
The mask is now removed, and Simon's picture of the same boulevard in the seventies vividly illustrates the dramatic contrast between Marlowe's world and Wine's.

Sex and its many exotic manifestations comprise only the most
colorful pieces in the mosaic of life-styles in contemporary Los
Angeles that is created in *Wild Turkey*. Wine's investigation takes
him to places as variegated as the Terminal Island prison and the
Fox studios in Hollywood, as colorful as La Guantanamera, a Cuban
restaurant, and the Pirates of the Caribbean ride at Disneyland, as
decadent as Hollywood Boulevard and as fashionable as the "studied
funkiness" of Topanga Canyon or the chic Chateau Marmont, where
the "atmosphere of polite decay" reverberates with the nonstop
reggae beat of a perpetual party. As modern as the picture of contemporary Los Angeles is, Wine's attitude is sometimes as old-

fashioned as Marlowe's. Driving along the Santa Ana Freeway, for example, Wine describes the ugliness of the landscape:

> The Santa Ana Freeway between Los Angeles and Anaheim is the missing tenth ring of Dante's Inferno—fifty miles of franchise food stands, used-car lots, discount furniture outlets, oil refineries, rubber factories and trailer parks—the kind of environment that would kill a prairie dog just to look at it.
>
> That afternoon I got it all in slow motion. The traffic was moving like corpuscles through a cholesterol-rotted artery. First came the grimy ramparts of Boyle Heights, then the badlands of Pico Rivera and the City of Commerce, antiseptic think tanks mixed with industrial power plants and cheap-jack motels. Then came the Orange County border with its pseudo-dairies and vanishing citrus groves, the rancid air smelling of ozone and Nixon.

Only fleeting reminders of the almost-vanished natural beauty of the area save him from despair:

> The rain had swept the sky clean and it had stayed that way, the coast of Catalina still visible to the right with the skyline of Long Beach up ahead, each building etched against the blue. I could even make out the larger yachts moored along the Gold Coast of Orange County, their multicolored banners waving proudly above the marinas. It was as if the gods had given the city a second chance, had erased the last forty years and told us we could try again. But we'd better not muck it up this time.

The sharply-detailed picture Simon paints of the Southern California setting, including its splendors and its decadence, furnishes a fascinating backdrop for the adventures of his contemporary hero.

In addition to the proliferation of sex shops, massage parlors, liberation institutes, et al., one other important consequence of the sexual revolution is dramatized in *Wild Turkey*—the changing attitudes toward women. Wine finds himself struggling (as Spenser did in *Promised Land*) to overcome his sexist prejudices, which first become evident in his conversation with Alora Vazquez as she prepares to leave for a three-month tour with the theatre group she directs. Wine admits to having trouble accepting the idea "that a woman was free to go off and do what she wanted, when she

wanted. As free as I was." He suspects Alora is right when she
accuses him of wanting a woman "strong at the beginning, but more
and more dependent on you as the relationship goes on. Like training a horse." Such prejudices are embarrassingly inconsistent in a
man of Wine's radical social and political beliefs, and he struggles to
raise his consciousness.

He is aided in his efforts by Nancy Hecht, who seizes several
opportunities to remind him of his decidedly unliberated views of
women. For example, when he first meets her at the door of her
husband's apartment just after he has discovered Hecht's body, he
attempts to prevent her from entering. She accuses him of treating
her differently because she is a woman: "What's the matter? You
think because I'm a woman I can't take bad news." He is forced
to admit she's right, that if she had been a man he would not have
hesitated telling her about Hecht's murder. Later, as he speculates
about the identity of Deborah Frank's killer, he unthinkingly assumes it is a man. Nancy reminds him that he has no justification
for his assumption, that it could as well be a woman. (Of course
she is right, since *she* is the murderer. Nevertheless, her lesson in
consciousness raising is well-taken by Wine, who notes that she is
beginning to sound more like Alora Vazquez all the time.) Even
Aunt Sonya makes a contribution by carrying a picket sign in front
of an orthodox synogogue with a message written in Yiddish: "Fight
Sexism Among The Orthodox. A Minyan Means Men And Women."
But the most painful challenge to his view occurs when Nancy,
admitting the murder of Deborah Frank, describes her reaction as
she was forced to witness her husband engage in sexual intercourse
with another woman. Despite their widely publicized open marriage,
Nancy confesses she has remained faithful to Hecht during their
marriage; her response to the reality of his sexual liberation was
blind jealous rage, an emotional rejoinder to the whole concept of
open marriage which forces Wine to reexamine his own jealous
attitudes toward the women in his life:

> Sexual liberation was a tough bastard. I knew that from my own
> experience, my own jealousy and possessiveness. I remembered
> how, when we were first married, I couldn't stand Suzanne's
> descriptions of other guys she had slept with and how, later, I
> was unable to allow Alora the freedom I took for myself. I

could always sense my own fear, even terror, of challenging those sexual preoccupations that had been welded to me since childhood, even harder to alter than the deepest needs for power and material possessions.

By portraying Wine's self-doubts, Simon conveys his vulnerability, adding an all-important dimension to his character. If he is to be a man of his time (as Simon obviously wishes him to be), then he must adjust to all the currents and issues of his time, not just the political ones. In depicting Wine's confused attitudes toward women, Simon follows the lead of Chandler, Macdonald, and Parker in using the detective novel for the purpose of illustrating the development of his hero as a human being.

Simon's characterization, more sure-handed in *Wild Turkey* than in *The Big Fix*, is based on an interesting technique: rather than invent characters, he "borrows" them, basing many of them on real-life models. First used in his portrayal of Howard Eppis in *The Big Fix*, he employs this technique much more extensively in *Wild Turkey*. The result is a kind of *roman à clef* mystery: Gunther Thomas is Hunter Thompson; Jock Hecht is Norman Mailer; Meyer Greenglass is Meyer Lansky. This technique invariably prompts a guessing game—if Jock Hecht is Norman Mailer, then who is Nancy Hecht? Or Deborah Frank? Or Cynthia Hardwick? Actually, the identification of the models for the characters is relatively unimportant, for they exist in the novel without any essential reference to their real-life counterparts. But the advantage to Simon is clear; since characterization is not his strongest skill, why not borrow characters? This not only provides him with interesting ready-made characters, it gives the knowing reader the added pleasure of detecting similarities between Simon's characters and their models. What Simon must be judged on, however, is his skill in re-creating the character, in making him come alive on the page, and for the most part he succeeds quite effectively.

The character of Jock Hecht, for example, benefits initially from the parallel with Norman Mailer, but it soon attains its own separate identity and stature in the novel. Hecht's first appearance in the novel confirms Gunther Thomas's description of him as "A man of Faustian lusts . . . excessive . . . restless . . . endlessly searching . . ." Our first impression of him comes from the overheard sound of his voice as he dictates into a tape recorder while making love to a pair of sociology students from UCLA:

> Freedom from shame, freedom from possession. . . . Freedom in the pursuit of ecstasy. That is what we sought. The three of us—a dark, languid woman below me, a small-boned blonde above. We moved together like a three-backed serpent, undulating, vibrating. I was transcendent, unfettered, swimming like a Maori tribesman into the outstretched arms of our primal matriarchy.

Hecht is such a vibrant life-force that his death is a real shock in the novel. Despite being dispatched so quickly, however, he continues to dominate the novel, and subsequent revelations about him only serve to increase the human dimensions of his character. When Wine ultimately concludes that Hecht really did commit suicide, he perceives his action as a chivalric gesture aimed at diverting attention from his wife's guilt in Deborah Frank's murder. And despite his single-minded dedication to self-gratification, Hecht's final message to Wine leads him to the missing tapes and results in the exposure of Attorney General Dichter.

If Hecht is Faustian, Gunther Thomas is Dionysian. With his glistening bald head, black eyepatch, and silver-studded motorcycle jacket, he is a whirling dervish of a character whose frenetic activity keeps Wine (and the novel) hopping. Author of a book on the Chicago Outlaws motorcycle gang (Hunter Thompson's was on the Hell's Angels), Thomas aims to write an article for *Rolling Stone* entitled, "Death and Vengeance: On the Case With Moses Wine." (Thompson's books and articles frequently begin, "Fear and Loathing . . ." Thomas also shares Thompson's celebrated penchant for pill-popping and Wild Turkey bourbon.) There isn't much depth to Thomas's character; his importance lies in the roles he plays: handling the tough-talking for Wine (unlike many of his predecessors, Wine doesn't go in much for wisecracks); filling the reader in on background (he has obviously read *The Big Fix*); initiating the action by introducing Wine to the Hecht case and then keeping it moving by confirming the identity of Meiko and uncovering the link between Dichter and the Cubans. If Wine ever needs an associate, and can find enough stamina to keep up with him, Thomas would be a natural.

Meyer Greenglass is a more original creation. A sickly old man dying of cancer, he reveals a shrewdness that Wine never suspects. From his prison cell, huddled in a blanket with a copy of *Barron's* business weekly across his lap, he understands the implications of the case, deduces certain conclusions, and deftly uses Wine to confirm his suspicions. He is able to lead Wine to Meiko's body simply by referring him to a *Variety* article about a filming delay due to an air conditioning failure on the set of the movie she was appearing in because, as he explains to Wine, "I know something from the old days about getting rid of bodies . . ." Wine feels like a dope at being "catechized by a gangster Socrates," especially when he realizes his efforts have unwittingly led to the death of the woman with whom he has fallen in love. His only consolation is that thanks to Greenglass and Hecht, he is able to expose political corruption in high places.

Admirers of *The Big Fix* will find nothing to disappoint them in *Wild Turkey*, an exciting and entertaining novel, and a most successful continuation of the Moses Wine series. Like Simon's first effort, it manages to modernize the genre by focusing on contemporary situations, fashions, life-styles, and social issues. But in handling of plot, inventiveness, and treatment of character, it represents a distinct advance in Simon's skill. The success of *Wild Turkey* demonstrates convincingly that the '75 Wine is of rare vintage indeed.

PEKING DUCK

"*Murder on The Orient Express* meets the Bamboo Curtain," is how one of the characters in *Peking Duck* (1979) describes Moses Wine's latest case. It is an apt description for the "People's Detective" finds himself in a baffling mystery in the far-off People's Republic of China: he must solve the theft of a priceless gold duck which has been stolen from a closely guarded room apparently by one of the fourteen members of the American tour group he is with. Wine is thrust into the middle of a political situation in a country whose language, customs, and culture are totally foreign to him. The result is a novel that combines the mysteries of the Orient with suspense and political intrigue to produce a fascinating concoction which represents a radical departure for the hard-boiled detective novel.

Since *The Big Fix*, Wine has attained a certain degree of fame and fortune: his picture has appeared in *Rolling Stone*; he is featured in a cover story in *Modern Times* magazine; he has just completed a personal injury case for which he was paid fifteen percent of the lawyer's fee, enough to buy an $8,000 silver Porsche. But instead of enjoying the fruits of his success, he feels guilty, a situation not helped by his Aunt Sonya who, hearing he has purchased what she scornfully calls a "Gestapomobile," asks, "Did you burn your SDS card when you bought your automobile registration?" The purchase of the Porsche is symptomatic of a crisis in Wine's life—approaching middle age. Now thirty-three, restless and confused about his future, he is searching for direction in his life. On the one hand, the Porsche bears witness to his professional success and, as he admits, "I figured if I was going to eat the forbidden fruit, I at least ought to take a good bite." But his old radicalism, with its disdain for such bourgeois items and its commitment to working for the betterment of society, asserts itself, producing guilt. It is normal for a private detective to experience periods of self-doubt, to question his fitness or desire to continue in his profession. But for most of his colleagues, such doubts normally arise from a sense of personal failure, from a distaste for violence, or simply from frustration at the pervasiveness of evil in the world. In Wine's case, doubts arise over the conflict between his politics and his profession—he wonders if his ex-wife is right when she says, "Someone who wrote a critique of More's *Utopia* like you did at Berkeley shouldn't spend all his life serving processes on runaway housewives"—and between his idealism and the temptations represented by such extravagant luxuries as his new silver Porsche. Wine is at a critical juncture in his life:

> The classic symptoms of incipient middle age were creeping up on me. I was bored and alienated. I had fantasies: Sometimes it was opening a bookstore in Berkeley. Sometimes it was joining the working class on the GM assembly line. Sometimes it was even going back and finishing law school. I didn't know what I wanted. All I knew was I wanted out.

So when Aunt Sonya invites him to join Friendship Study Tour Number Five to the People's Republic of China (of which she is group leader), he seizes the opportunity, even though he recognizes that going to China with Sonya would be like "going on a tour of the Vatican with Saint Bernadette."

In *Peking Duck*, Simon makes explicit what has been implicit in his previous novels—Wine's ambivalence about his profession and discomfort at his success—as well as what is implicit in the hard-boiled novel itself, at least since Chandler—the use of the private detective's investigation as an occasion for self-examination. When Lew Archer accepts a case where he searches for a lost son, or when Spenser labors to save the career of a professional baseball player, each becomes involved in a situation which mirrors his personal concerns, and solution of the problem compels self-examination because of personal investment in the case. By the same token, Wine's trip to China offers more than a convenient opportunity to get away from it all for a while; it becomes a kind of spiritual journey:

> No matter how lightly I took it, whatever wisecracks I made, going to China for me was not like taking a trip to New York or London, or even to Tokyo or Bombay. It was a search for self, a search for values that were waning so fast I wondered if I ever had them. After fifteen years of flirting around radical movements, playing footsy with commitment, I wanted to find out if it was worth resolving the ambivalence in my life, an ambivalence which had reduced whatever idealism I had left to copping attitudes at cocktail parties and making donations at liberal fund raisers. And if there was a resolution, I thought it would be in China, the one place where the egalitarian ideal did not seem to have been completely vitiated by self-serving bureaucrats and distinctly non-socialist expansionism. At least not yet.

The first thing he realizes, however, is that his spiritual pilgrimage won't be made alone but in the company of a radical-chic ship of fools. The fourteen-member Friendship Study Tour includes, among others, Ruby Crystal, a China-loving movie actress, Staughton Grey, a radical hero of Wine's whose speech at the Cooper Union in 1958 prompted him to join his first peace group at the age of fifteen, Nick Spitzler, the radical attorney Wine consulted in *The Big Fix* (film version), Ana Tzu and Li Yu-ying, expatriated Chinese, and Harvey Walsh, director of "the Personal Growth Gestalt Instalt Institute of Santa Barbara," who arrives at the predeparture party at Ruby Crystal's with foam clubs for the members of the group to hit each other and release tension before the trip. Like Wine, each person has his own reason for visiting China: for some, like Ana Tzu, Li Yu-ying, and Fred Lisle, a professor of Asian Studies, it is a return to the country of their birth; for Mike Sanchez, the only working-class member of the group, a chance to observe the effects of revolution on the lives of the workers; for Reed Hadley, a financial investment, since he hopes to make a large profit from the buying and selling of Chinese art.

Wine's desire to escape his profession is immediately threatened when the husband of Nancy Lemon, a member of the group, takes him aside at the Los Angeles airport and tries to hire him to spy on his wife's sexual activities during the trip. Wine refuses, unwilling to sully his spiritual journey with any professional responsibilities. (Wine is so committed to the spiritual nature of his sojourn that he even declines the invitation of a Hong Kong prostitute because, he explains, when he enters the People's Republic, "I want to go pure.") Nevertheless, he cannot suppress for long his detective instincts, especially when several unusual events occur on the trip. First, in Hong Kong some Chinese knock on his door looking for Ana Tzu, who later mysteriously becomes ill and remains behind when the group moves on to Canton. In Canton, a man falls to his death from a grain storage bin at a commune the Americans are visiting. Wine is suspicious about the gash on the back of the man's head and curious about the particularly pained reaction of Mrs. Liu, an attractive Chinese guide who has been assigned to their group. Ana Tzu rejoins the tour in Canton but is stricken again and forced to remain behind once more when the others proceed to Shanghai, where the Americans are attacked by several Chinese youth, who hurl rocks and insults at them. The Chinese authorities are apologetic about these unpleasant events, but they are also displeased over rumors about the Americans' behavior. They are upset that one of the group apparently attempted to climb over the wall of the *Liberation Daily* newspaper after being denied admission. Also, the report that Fred Lisle has requested permission to share a room with Nancy Lemon disturbs the puritanical Chinese. When the Americans are subjected to another attack by what the Chinese describe as "bad elements," supporters of the now discredited "Gang of Four" (a group of radicals led by Chiang Ching, Mao Tse-tung's wife), which is committed to ideological purity, the authorities decide that the Americans should proceed immediately to Peking, two days earlier than scheduled.

Once in Peking, the plans are abruptly changed again. Citing the unpleasant incidents and the group's negative attitude, the Chinese officials announce that it would be in the best interest of both parties for the Americans to leave China the next day. As a final gesture of friendship, however, the group is invited to be the first foreigners granted admission to the Garden of the Western Flowers, which has been closed to the public for several years. The Americans gladly accept and are dazzled by the beauty of the display, especially the prize item—a two-thousand-year-old Han Dynasty duck crafted of gold with carved carnelian feet and delicate white jade feathers. Unearthed in 1968 in Manching, Hopi province, it was the most valuable of all the archeological finds, so valuable that it was not permitted to leave China as part of the exhibition of items which toured the United States. The euphoria at being allowed a view of this exquisite duck quickly fades a few hours later when security officials announce that the group will not be leaving China the next day as planned: the priceless duck is missing, and all indications point to one of the Americans as the thief.

The theft gives every appearance of being a typical locked-room mystery. An object is stolen from a closely guarded room to which only a group of Americans and their Chinese guides have been allowed access. None of the Chinese would have stolen it, the authorities explain, because in an egalitarian society like China's, nobody would be foolish enough to steal an object nobody else had. On the other hand, several of the Americans appear to have very strong motives for stealing the duck: Reed Hadley, who has been "acting like the China representative of every antique store west of New Jersey," has been obsessed with the duck since the trip began; Ruby Crystal, the actress, already owns the largest collection of Oriental art on the West Coast; Fred Lisle, a missionary's son born in China, might have chosen to strike back at godless China in this way; Li Yu-ying's father lost everything—two factories, a couple of houses—when the Communists took over; Natalie Levine has a $100,000 debt from her recent unsuccessful Senate campaign, and the duck would fetch more than enough to cover that. Even Wine himself comes under suspicion when the Chinese intercept a money order for $15,000 sent to him by Nancy Lemon's husband. His explanation that it was payment for a job he never accepted (spying on Nancy Lemon) is not entirely convincing.

Fortunately, Wine discovers he has been unable to turn off the switch that makes him a detective, and as he instinctively begins reviewing the case he discovers his uncertainties about his profession begin to disappear. He now begins to suspect that his previous ambivalence about his work was nothing more than self-pity, "what they would call here in China petit bourgeois vacillation," and concludes that "to look for the truth beneath surfaces was an honorable profession, a worthwhile endeavor given the choices we have, even in the tawdry clothes of the private dick." Since this is a case where neither money nor celebrity status is a factor, the challenge is pure and simple: discover the truth and rescue his fellow Americans from their embarrassing (and terrifying) situation. It has taken a trip halfway around the world to rekindle his desire to act as a private detective again and to test the Maoist lesson he is taught by Liu, his beautiful Communist guide: "If you first learn to serve the people, if you learn to *need* to serve them, then you will be an expert at what you do. You will do it better because you do it for the right reason."

Wine receives a mysterious phone call telling him, "Right now go bright and flowery." He procures an address for the "bright and flowery," discovers it to be a Chinese bathhouse, and is surprised to find there one of the "bad elements" who attacked the group in Shanghai. He follows him when he leaves and narrowly escapes with his life when the youth turns and lunges at him with a knife. Wine's close call, coupled with the phone message, leads him to conclude there is more to the case than the simple theft of the duck, but his confidence isn't helped any by his realization that instead of the mean streets of Los Angeles, he is walking the dangerous and very foreign streets of Peking: "I had never felt so out of my element in my life. Indeed, I had never *been* so out of my element in my life." Nevertheless, he reaches one conclusion that solves a crucial part of the mystery: he guesses correctly that it was Liu who took the duck. But why?

Wine pressures her to accompany him to Shanghai, where he hopes to uncover the mystery of the "bad elements"; on the way she admits she stole the duck in order to detain the group and secure his help in exposing her fellow guide, Yen, who, she says, is an agent of the Taiwanese dedicated to discrediting the People's Republic in the eyes of foreign visitors in order to sabotage normalization between China and the United States. Several of the earlier incidents—the attacks of the "bad elements," the false reports about the Americans' behavior, the phone call about the "bright and flowery"—were apparently fabricated by Yen to disrupt the tour. Liu explains she needs Wine's help because she believes Yen has an American confederate in the group, and she also knows the Chinese authorities would not believe her accusations because for seven years, she now admits, she was personal translator for Chiang Ching, leader of the hated "Gang of Four" blamed for all of China's current ills. Liu's ploy works; she succeeds in enlisting Wine's support, but she warns him to be careful, citing the death of the man at the commune who, she also now reveals, was working with her.

When they reach Shanghai, Wine leaves her behind and makes his way to the place where the Americans were first attacked by the "bad elements." Surprised to hear the totally unexpected but very familiar sound of Elvis Presley's voice, he approaches cautiously and is stunned at the amazing scene before him—a juke-box, rock and roll music playing, couples doing the twist, all in all a "weird time-warp, half pre-revolutionary China, half 1959 sock hop." Unfortunately, he doesn't notice Yen, who appears behind him with a gun and invites him to join his fellow American private detective inside, nodding to a poster of Bogart in *The Big Sleep* hanging on the wall. Yen and his Chinese friends are secret devotees of American culture, counter-revolutionaries inspired by the fifties music of such rock and roll singers as Gene Vincent and Buddy Holly to undermine what Yen describes as the stultifying boredom of the Chinese Communist culture:

> You do not understand what it is like here. Any of you. You do not know what it means—every day the same, getting up and working hour after hour, the same way, the same place, like a slave, for some myth of serving the people that only exists over the loudspeaker!

Now that he has Wine, he decides to use him for his own purposes. Explaining that his American contact has delivered only $2,000 of a promised $10,000, he wants Wine to get the rest of the money. And he wants the missing duck. In return he offers as payment the life of Liu, whose drugged body he now produces. Yen explains to Wine that he should have little trouble obtaining the duck because under the influence of sodium pentathol Liu has revealed its location—Aunt Sonya now has it.

Wine finds himself far more deeply entangled in politics than he ever was in *The Big Fix*, and he is distressed at how high the stakes have risen. He knows he might be able to free the Americans if he returns the duck to the Chinese authorities, but such an action will certainly insure Liu's death, and because of his growing attraction to her he cannot allow that to happen. Besides, the future of Chinese-American relations is at stake. So he decides to take an enormous risk: He returns to Peking and retrieves the duck from Sonya, then makes his way to the speaker's platform in Tien An Men Square where, before a crowd of a million Chinese gathered to celebrate the Eleventh Party Congress, he holds the duck aloft and shouts, "Long Live Chiang Ching! Long Live the 'Gang of Four'!" He is immediately arrested and two days later placed on trial for counter-revolutionary activities.

Wine has succeeded in his plan to draw attention to the case, but the Chinese authorities are unmoved by his wild accusations against Yen, a loyal guide for the China Travel Service for fourteen years. Wine realizes his only hope of discrediting Yen is to reveal publicly the identity of his American confederate who, he has learned from Sonya, is none other than his radical hero, Staughton Grey. (Sonya also reveals that Grey was the lover she abandoned forty years earlier when she discovered he was a government agent. Because of their love, Grey interceded on her behalf and she was the only member of the Communist group she belonged to in the Bronx who was not arrested. Now, still harboring a love for him, she cannot bring herself to expose him as a C.I.A. agent. Hence, she arranged with Liu, whom she has known for several years, to have Wine included on this trip so he could smoke Grey out if necessary.) Grey, who is attending the trial, is nonplussed at Wine's gambit but, recognizing his cover has been blown, he accepts the bait and announces he is ready to make a self-criticism, thereby substantiating

Wine's accusations. Liu is saved, the threat to normalization between the People's Republic and the United States is removed, and the Americans are free to leave the country. How ironic that the Han Dynasty Duck, a relic of China's Imperial past, becomes the means of saving Communist China from the counter-revolutionary activities of Yen and his Taiwanese associates.

Peking Duck is a multi-faceted novel, part travelogue, part political primer, part mystery. In 1977, Simon spent a month in China, and the novel obviously reflects his views of the country and its people, customs, attitudes, and politics. Canton, Peking, and the legendary and colorful Shanghai are all vividly portrayed. Simon also uses Wine's journey through China to depict many of the changes wrought by the Communist Revolution: in the New China, for example, a prison is transformed into a child care center, a lavish old whorehouse becomes a Children's Palace. Cultural distinctions between the Chinese and the Americans, such as differing attitudes toward sexual behavior, material possessions, the open expression of emotion, and the role of popular music, are explored. The tantalizing descriptions of several meals Wine and his fellow Americans enjoy would make Spenser's mouth water. Simon also manages to weave a good deal of Chinese political history into the book, especially current attitudes toward the excesses of the infamous "Gang of Four," although Wine finally has to admit that the conflicting reports of Mao's attitudes toward his wife Chiang Ching, leader of the "Gang of Four," comprised "a thicket of hearsay as dense as eighteen-and-a-half minutes of twisted Watergate tape— and twice as long." Wine's arrest even allows Simon to incorporate information about China's legal system, with its two different types of trials: one for "Contradictions Among the People," the other, Wine's, for "Contradictions Between the People and the Enemy."

However, to accomplish all these things, Simon has had to de-emphasize plot, not necessarily a bad thing, especially since his plots in both *The Big Fix* and *Wild Turkey* tended to be overly complicated. When Liu asks Wine if he reads detective novels, he says not often because "they usually sacrifice everything to the plot," a statement which appears to reflect Simon's view, at least as it applies to *Peking Duck*, where plot is clearly subservient to other matters. However, in reducing plot complexity and importance,

Simon falls into the same trap Parker did in *Promised Land*, where overemphasis on character, theme, and other discursive elements resulted in a sluggish narrative and diminished tension and surprise. The plot of *Peking Duck* moves slowly, the first third of the novel largely introduction to such matters as Wine's personal crisis, the personalities of the various members of the tour group, and the current political situation in China. The actual crime in the novel—theft of the duck—doesn't occur until chapter sixteen. Once this takes place, the pace picks up noticeably, and the action and suspense propel the narrative to its dramatic conclusion. However, the languid pace of the first third of the novel threatens to alienate the reader's attention. The material presented is informative, and Simon manages to tease the reader by interjecting such mysteries as Ana Tzu's sudden illness (which turns out to be nothing more than an excuse she concocts in order to remain behind in Canton for an extended visit with relatives) and the dramatic death of the man at the commune (although we never learn any more details about the incident other than that he was working with Liu). *Peking Duck* exposes certain weaknesses that seem to accompany experimentation to find the often elusive balance between action and exposition, between tightly knit plot and in-depth exploration of theme.

One positive result of Simon's diminished emphasis on plot in *Peking Duck* is a fuller, more sharply etched portrait of Wine's character as he strives to resolve his ambivalence over his career, and remove the contradiction he notes between his professional activities and his political beliefs. Is he, he wonders, really dedicated to the people, or is he only, as he refers to himself, a "parlour Maoist from the Hollywood Hills," and "something of a left-wing voyeur?" Firsthand observation of the day-to-day reality of the Chinese Communist system helps him clarify his own beliefs. There are many things he admires in Chinese society: its egalitarianism; the spirit and pride of the people; the lack of emphasis on material possessions. Above all, he loves to watch the children playing games on the principle of "Friendship first, competition second." As he observes them, his thoughts turn to his own children: "I wished they were there, wished children everywhere could grow up in a world where, from the age of two, they were taught to share and love each other as much as themselves. This—these children—was the beauty and the glory of the New China." And yet his experience in China also convinces him that he is too much an individualist to accept the restrictions he sees placed on the individual. There is, among other things, no place for a private detective in such a communal society. Yen's complaint about the oppressive boredom of life in China also strikes a responsive chord, and Wine concludes that he values his individuality too much to submerge himself in the group; "Maybe I just couldn't make the leap into serving the people," he finally admits. He doesn't fully solve the dilemma of the Porsche, but when he decides to sell it at the end of the novel, it isn't because of any newly found commitment to nonmaterial values; the repair bills are simply too expensive.

An important contribution to Wine's education is made by Mrs. Liu who, like Nancy Hecht in *Wild Turkey* (and like Susan Silverman in Parker's novels), prompts him to reexamine his attitudes. Liu is a beautiful woman with "bright hazel eyes and a pale yellow complexion that was absolutely exquisite, like a bead of unblemished amber held up to the light," and it isn't long before Wine finds himself, despite the many warnings against it, lusting for her, a "veritable Jimmy Carter practicing adultery in my mind." But, like Nancy Hecht, she too turns out to be the criminal he is looking for although hers is a political crime designed to promote the cause of the Chinese people. Liu, a dedicated Communist who reads Hegel and Chairman Mao in her spare time, does nothing to ease Wine's doubts about his shaky commitment to the principles of revolution when she charges him with being a "cynical, self-serving person" who demonstrates "no need to serve the people of any country." She even accuses him, with some truth, of a kind of revolutionary dilettantism, charging that "not everyone has the money or the time to travel all around the world studying other people's revolutions." And before she finally succumbs to his advances, endangering her own career by making love with him on the train to Shanghai, she sees fit to lecture him; she accuses him of being a member of a "reactionary ruling class elite" whose mind has "been infected by the disease of materialism" and who is interested in her, in part at least, because she is a symbol of the New China, "a society so much more moral than your own." Wine bristles at her overweening patriotism and stagy rhetoric, but he remains impressed by her unwavering commitment to the principles of revolution. And her complaints at least have the effect of forcing him to explain to her (and defend to himself) his own shaky attitudes and beliefs.

His endeavor to redefine his political beliefs is reminiscent of Spenser's similar efforts in *Mortal Stakes* and *Promised Land* to clarify his own principles. Both Wine and Spenser seek to establish personal codes of conduct, but what in Spenser's case involves reconciling his violent actions with his ethical principles, in Wine's involves satisfying his political rather than his moral conscience. The fact that both characters fail to resolve their dilemmas completely serves only to make them more human as characters. Ambiguity, uncertainty, and self-doubt haunt the private detective wherever he goes because he not only must establish his authenticity as a man, he must also reaffirm his commitment to a profession which lies at the fringe of society. The private detective is fundamentally an outsider with one foot in, one foot outside, his society. The challenge is to maintain the balance without toppling to either side. Not only does his choice of profession place Wine outside the mainstream of society; his social and political views are more radical than those held by the majority of his fellow countrymen. He strives to hold onto those views, although his experience in China convinces him he is not ready to go so far as to surrender his individuality in order to embrace the classlessness of communist society. In other words, he isn't yet ready to give up the Porsche. That he doesn't successfully resolve his dilemma is not important; that he is willing to face it, is.

If there is a flaw in Wine's characterization, it is that he is not entirely convincing as a topnotch private detective. In *The Big Fix*, he initially established his credentials by solving the mystery of Howard Eppis and thwarting Oscar Procari's attempt to sabotage the California primary election. But in *Wild Turkey*, he is little more than a pawn in the crafty hands of Meyer Greenglass, who actually directs the investigation from his prison cell, with Wine only verifying his suspicions about the murder of his niece. And again in *Peking Duck*, Wine finds himself duped, this time by his Aunt Sonya, who conspires with her Chinese friend Liu to get him on this particular trip to China in order to use him to expose Yen's subversive activities. Although he thinks he is working to solve the mystery of the missing duck, he is actually a key figure in a matter of international intrigue, thanks to Liu. Despite all the publicity he has received as the "Gumshoe of the Sixties Generation," and his widely known reputation as "The People's Detective," in those cases which are depicted in the novels he does not impress the reader as a particularly shrewd operator, although this in no way diminishes interest in him as a character. It merely reinforces the notion that Simon is primarily interested in Wine as a survivor of the radical sixties with a variety of social and political hang-ups to overcome rather than as a defender of the innocent or savior of the helpless, knightly roles enacted by many of his predecessors.

Peking Duck shares with Parker's most recent novel, *The Judas Goat*, a radical shift away from the traditional American urban setting for the hard-boiled novel, although Simon goes even further than Parker does. Where the European setting of *The Judas Goat* provides little more than a fresh backdrop for Spenser's latest adventure, the Chinese setting is inextricably related to the mystery in *Peking Duck*; indeed, the case could not take place elsewhere, and Wine comes as close as one could imagine to operating as a Chinese private detective, a kind of occidental Charlie Chan. Simon has chosen to continue his modernization of the genre by placing his hero in a situation with as much contemporary impact as today's newspaper headlines, notably the tentatively evolving relationship between China and the United States. At the same time, he continues his interesting exploration into the consciousness of Wine, disclosing new aspects of his character.

3

Andrew Bergman

Andrew Bergman was born in New York City on February 20, 1945, the son of German refugees. His father, Rudy Bergman, was for many years a radio and television critic for *The New York Daily News*. Following graduation from Harpur College in Binghamton, New York in 1965, Bergman attended the University of Wisconsin, earning a Ph.D. in American Intellectual History in 1970. In 1973, he married Louise Fay, and they have one child, Jacob Max, born in 1978. Bergman and his family reside in New York City.

Unable to obtain a teaching position, Bergman worked for a year in the publicity department of United Artists in New York after leaving graduate school. During this time, he wrote a novella, *Tex X*, about the adventures of a contemporary black man in the Old West. Although never published, the story became the basis for the popular film, *Blazing Saddles*, a comic parody of Western movies, which he coauthored with Mel Brooks and Richard Pryor. In 1971, he published *We're In the Money* (the subject of his doctoral dissertation at Wisconsin), a study of American films of the thirties and how they maintained national morale during the Depression by emphasizing stories of aspiration and optimism. His interest in film history also resulted in a biography of James Cagney, published in 1973. Since 1975, Bergman has devoted his efforts to screenwriting. His first script, *Rhapsody in Crime* (as yet unproduced), a comic epic which imitates features of the classic gangster film, was purchased by Warner Brothers. Another film of his, *The In-Laws*, was released in 1979 to considerable critical and popular acclaim.

It wasn't until 1971, while on vacation in Jamaica, that Bergman read his first Raymond Chandler novel and, as he describes it, "went berserk." Sparked by Chandler's brilliantly imaginative use of language, he began writing an imitation of the 1940s detective novel. However, as the book developed, his interest in history quickly asserted itself, and by the time the novel, *The Big Kiss-Off of 1944*, with private detective Jack LeVine, was published in 1974, it had become far more substantial than a simple exercise in comic invention. This shift from parody to a more serious purpose is even more apparent in the second Jack LeVine novel, *Hollywood and LeVine*, published in 1975, which Bergman maintains is "in no manner, shape, or form a parody." Like Simon, Bergman considers his detective novels as something more than simple mysteries. "I never really saw myself as a mystery writer," he concludes. "I saw myself simply as a writer who was using that form. My novels are really historical novels."

THE BIG KISS-OFF OF 1944

If mystery writers like Robert Parker and Roger Simon can be said to be the rightful heirs to the Hammett-Chandler-Macdonald tradition of the hard-boiled novel, then those writers whose work can best be described as parody are its illegitimate children. These bastard sons resemble their famous fathers in many respects, yet they can be distinguished from their more legitimate siblings by their frequently irreverent, sometimes downright disrespectful, attitudes. However, despite lacking full claims to legitimacy, they command attention for their natural charm and disarming cleverness in striving so hard to be taken as seriously as their more estimable brethren.

All writers of hard-boiled fiction since Hammett have been imitators of the genre; a writer of parody, however, is a comic imitator, one who consciously seeks to impersonate rather than innovate. Parody is a tricky literary technique. At its most extreme, it is little more than a comic spoof of a literary work. One of the

first (and still one of the wittiest) parodies of the hard-boiled novel
is S. J. Perelman's "Farewell, My Lovely Appetizer," an ingenious
imitation of the style and conventions of the classic private-eye
novel. But parody as an end in itself is a form of decadence, art
feeding off art. Since its primary purpose is humor at the expense
of the original, it deserves little consideration in any serious study
of the hard-boiled genre.

However, done in a different spirit, with enough talent and
imagination, parody can serve a far more fruitful purpose. Rather
than employing parody simply as an end in itself, a number of
writers have discovered the advantage of using parody to advance
their more serious objectives as writers. In the 1970s there was an
outpouring of works which depend for their effect, to one degree or
another, on a knowledge of the classic hard-boiled novel and which
imitate many of its most characteristic features. In addition to films,
both serious (*Chinatown*) and comic (*The Black Bird, The Cheap
Detective*), and countless television series, there have been novels
by such diverse writers as Thomas Berger (*Who Is Teddy Villanova?*), Richard Brautigan (*Dreaming of Babylon*), John Gregory
Dunne (*True Confessions*), William Hjortsberg (*Falling Angel*),
and Stuart Kaminsky (*Bullet For A Star, Murder On The Yellow
Brick Road, You Bet Your Life*). Their intentions differ widely, but
all of them share in common a return to the past for inspiration, and
each of the novels depends upon a familiarity with the genre, employs some variation of the tough-talking narrator/hero, and imitates the classic hard-boiled style.

One of the most successful of these writers is Andrew Bergman,
who manages to combine the comic effects of parody with a seriousness of purpose, an affection for the genre, and his own considerable
talents as a mystery writer to produce in *The Big Kiss-Off of 1944*
(1974) and *Hollywood and LeVine* (1975) two inventive examples
of how parody, handled skillfully, can enliven rather than denigrate
the genre. One expects parody to be entertaining, and Bergman's
novels are that. But by keeping the parodic elements under tight
control, he manages to evoke a sense of the past in writing what
amounts to forties mystery novels. While one cannot go so far as to
say his novels are as satisfying as discovering a previously unknown
Raymond Chandler mystery, they are accomplished and inventive
enough to satisfy the most demanding aficionado of the period.

Bergman manages the almost impossible task of sounding like a contemporary of Chandler.

The easist thing to parody (although difficult to do well) is the hard-boiled style, and Bergman does an excellent job of capturing its essential features. It was Chandler who gave the hard-boiled novel its distinctive sound by embellishing Hammett's tough-guy prose with colorful similes, barbed wisecracks, comic exaggerations, and witty dialogue. Consequently, most stylistic parodies of the genre are really parodies of Chandler's style and mannerisms. (Chandler himself was occasionally guilty of self-parody.) One of the most distinctive features of his style is the use of striking similes, and Bergman captures this flavor frequently in *The Big Kiss-Off of 1944* in such examples as these: a two-bit gangster LeVine disarms is described as "looking like a dog caught crapping on the rug"; LeVine and a distinguished Philadelphia banker, trying to pass in disguise through a group of men looking for them, walk "about as casually as two priests in a strip joint"; two thugs staking out LeVine's apartment "stuck out like hard-ons in a Turkish bath." Chandler's prospensity for comic hyperbole is also captured by Bergman: a Broadway producer's office is so large "you could have run the Kentucky Derby" in it, the couches so big "the Yankees could have fit on [them] comfortably"; a burly policeman has "shoulders you could use for a dance floor"; a man has such lousy marksmanship "he couldn't hit Kate Smith at three feet." Chandler's witty dialogue also finds its echoes in *The Big Kiss-Off of 1944*. For example, when a not-so-bright character remarks to LeVine that it is so quiet "You can hear yourself think," LeVine replies, "Can you hear anything?" Or when a caller tells LeVine he doesn't wish to discuss his case over the phone, he cracks, "Well, that's fine by me. How about leaning out your window and shouting it over?"

These stylistic echoes are immensely entertaining, yet they do not exist for their own sake. Bergman keeps them under control, thus avoiding the temptation to exaggerate them too outrageously simply for the sake of humor. He aims to recapture the tone of the forties style without ridiculing it, and he labors to keep such stylistic mannerisms consistent with the character of his hero, whom he does not wish to turn into a comic character. It is here where a critical distinction can be made between Bergman and, say, Thomas Berger, whose *Who Is Teddy Villanova?*, brilliant though it is, is primarily a parody of the hard-boiled style which depends for its comic effects on linguistic exaggeration and non-stop mimicry. Bergman employs just enough of the verbal idiom to capture the appropriate tone without endangering the realism of the character of LeVine, for whom he has serious plans.

Jack LeVine ("Like Hollywood and Vine") has changed his name from Jacob Levine, but that is about the only concession to glamour he makes. He describes himself as a "basic 1944 prole," an average guy who likes his beer ("No law of man or nature would stop me from having an ice-cold beer every afternoon of my adult life"), his poker (although he plays poorly because he smiles whenever he gets a good hand), and his baseball. Physically, he fails to measure up to the stereotyped image of the private detective hero: he is bald (although he admits, "I don't look half-bad when I keep my hat on"), tends to perspire heavily, and is woefully out of shape ("I'm thirty-eight and have the body of a fifty-year-old"). Like Lew Archer and Moses Wine, he is divorced (his wife decided "she'd be better off married to someone who came home three nights out of five and had an even chance of making it past fifty") but has a girl friend named Kitty Seymour, although one would hardly describe their relationship as passionate (they have slept together only once in six months, although their average improves during the course of the novel). He works out of a shabby office on the ninth floor of a building on Broadway and 52nd Street and lives in a small apartment in Sunnyside, Queens.

In his choice of profession, he has rejected the fur business his father had gotten stuck in and has disappointed his mother, who hoped her only son would become a dentist. However, he harbors no romantic illusions about being a private detective; at times he considers himself only a "shmendrick getting paid by big people to do ugly work," and cynically describes his job this way: "I followed people around for a living, I looked for used condoms in the trash." He is realistic enough to know he cannot live up to any glamorous Dick Tracy image; he is the kind of detective, for example, who admits to getting diarrhea on a stakeout. And concerning his powers of deduction, he says wryly, "Show me [room] 801 and I'll find 805 two times out of three." Moreover, LeVine gives little thought to the noble role of knight errant that Marlowe, Archer, and Spenser frequently saw themselves playing. He is just a "Jew shamus" trying to prove he can cut the mustard. Nevertheless, despite his self-deprecating attitude, LeVine is every bit their equal when it comes to shrewdness, honesty, integrity, and commitment, qualities which are severely tested in *The Big Kiss-Off of 1944.*

The plot of the novel parallels elements of Parker's *Mortal Stakes* and Simon's *The Big Fix*, with an affectionate nod to Chandler's *The Big Sleep* thrown in. (It is surely no coincidence that the titles of the initial mystery efforts of both Simon and Bergman echo Chandler's first novel, *The Big Sleep.*) It is early summer, 1944, when a beautiful blonde enters LeVine's office and sits down under the War Bonds poster. She identifies herself as Kerry Lane, a chorus girl who has come to hire him to stop a man named Duke Fenton from blackmailing her because of some stag films she once made. Exposure, she fears, will cost her her job in the Broadway musical she is currently appearing in. LeVine agrees to take the case, but when he arrives at Fenton's hotel room, he discovers he has just been murdered. Later that day, LeVine receives a phone call from Warren Butler, producer of the Broadway show Kerry Lane is in, who wants to hire him to stop whoever is blackmailing *him* by threatening to expose the identity of one of his chorus girls (who LeVine knows to be Kerry Lane) who has reportedly appeared in a stag film. LeVine goes to the Smithtown, Long Island address the blackmailer gave Butler but finds the place deserted. At 3:00 A.M. the next morning, the missing blackmailer, who identifies himself as Al Rubine, shows up at LeVine's apartment, obviously frightened, and convinces him to drive him upstate where he promises to deliver the stag films. On the way, their car is stopped by two patrolmen, one of whom knocks LeVine unconscious. When he awakens, he discovers Rubine missing; later, he learns his body has been found stuffed into a nearby drainpipe.

In less than forty-eight hours, LeVine has been hired by two different people to stop two different blackmailers, both of whom end up murdered. Obviously, he is onto something big here. But what? He remembers seeing a newspaper photograph on the floor of Rubine's deserted hideout which showed New York Governor Thomas E. Dewey (about to be nominated as the Republican candidate for president of the United States) shaking hands with a man identified as Eli W. Savage, president of the Quaker National Bank in Philadelphia, so he decides to question Savage. He takes the train to Philadelphia and, posing as a building inspector, manages to gain access to the fire escape outside Savage's office. Suddenly, shots ring out and he realizes someone is shooting at him. He dives through Savage's window and who should he find in his office but Kerry Lane, who confesses she is actually Anne Savage, daughter of the prominent banker. Savage explains that he is a principal contributor to and fund-raiser for Dewey's upcoming Presidential bid; the blackmailers are threatening to expose his daughter's "acting" background and ruin his reputation unless he stays away from the Dewey campaign. Someone wants him out of the picture and since LeVine is conveniently standing there in his office, he offers him $2500 to find out who it is.

LeVine returns to New York and before long receives a phone call from a man who identifies himself as General Redlin, summoning him to a breakfast meeting the following morning at the Waldorf Towers hotel. When he arrives, he sees so many plainclothesmen and security officials milling about that he wonders if "maybe a lot of people had died and I was now the President of the United States." Not quite, but he does find himself in the company of some of President Roosevelt's closest advisors: generals, colonels, admirals, an impressive array of Army and Navy brass. Also, Lee Factor, a political hatchet man for FDR ("He would light your cigarette while the firing squad took aim"), and Warren Butler, the Broadway producer who had earlier hired him to find the blackmailer. It turns out that *these* men—all loyal supporters of FDR dedicated to securing his reelection—are the blackmailers. One of the colonels claims that Roosevelt's reelection is essential to the successful conclusion of the war effort and argues that the defeat of Dewey is a defense priority. With Butler's help, they have obtained the films Anne Savage once made, and are using them to keep her father from contributing to Dewey's campaign. All they want from LeVine is his cooperation in getting off the case. General Redlin's appeal to LeVine's patriotism fails, partly because, like Moses Wine, he is apolitical ("I don't like Dewey," he explains, "but I don't like extortion either. My politics are strictly for LeVine. I don't care if Attila the Hun wins this November."), partly because he is disgusted by the actions of Factor and his cronies, especially when he learns they had Fenton and Rubine killed for attempting to make a little extra cash by blackmailing Anne Savage on their own. When General Redlin stoops to flattery, praising him as "a man who loves his country," LeVine blows up: "That's priceless, general, really. You love your country so much you can put the squeeze on a twenty-year-old girl for making a not-very-terrible mistake, and you can stick some schlemiel of a crook head first into a drainpipe. If that's patriotism then I'm Tokyo Rose." He angrily walks out on the assembled group of distinguished blackmailers and murders, feeling "clearly superior to every other living creature" for having withstood their relentless cajolery.

LeVine's principles are tested again the next day when Lee Factor visits his office to up the ante: he offers LeVine a briefcase containing $25,000 cash and guarantees him that the IRS will not audit his taxes no matter how low he pegs his income. LeVine again refuses. (Like most of his colleagues, he can be hired but not bought.) Factor becomes desperate and, claiming that "The re-election of the president is the only thing that makes a damn bit of difference . . . Anything that returns him to the White House is worth it, is moral, is justifiable," he pulls a gun and fires at him. Only his wretched marksmanship saves LeVine, who knocks Factor out and then puts him (and his $25,000) in a taxi and sends him back to the Waldorf Towers.

Sitting on the toilet in his apartment reading a newspaper story about Dewey's nomination at the Republican convention in Chicago, LeVine appreciates the seriousness of the situation and enjoys a certain amount of satisfaction in knowing that "the chunky man taking a Sunnyside shit was a mover and shaker of world events." Just how important he is becomes evident when Savage calls and invites him to a private meeting with the newly nominated Republican candidate, Thomas E. Dewey himself. (Roger Simon demonstrated the advantage of basing characters on real life models; Bergman goes even further by using actual characters in his fiction.) Dewey has become suspicious after learning the New York police have been pulled off the investigation into the murders of Fenton and Rubine, apparently by political higher-ups, and he wants to know what LeVine knows.

LeVine finds himself in much the same position Moses Wine did in *The Big Fix*—he has an opportunity to influence an important election, the outcome of which is of little personal interest to him. He can pocket a cool $25,000 by simply sitting back and doing nothing. Or, if he chooses, he can tell Dewey what he knows about Factor's plan and insure his election by giving the Republicans an unbeatable campaign issue against the Democrats. Instead he follows his own personal ethics, which dictate that he do only what he was hired to do in the first place—protect Eli Savage's name and his daughter's reputation. Like Spenser in his attitude toward Linda Rabb in *Mortal Stakes*, LeVine doesn't think it right that Anne Savage should be made to pay for an unfortunate episode in her past: "She got caught in a mistake, not an uncommon one for rich girls who want to experience the world a little, who get bored with having everything done for them." He is also impressed by her loyalty in attempting to protect her father's name by concealing the fact that she was Eli Savage's daughter when she hired him. LeVine's commitment is clear. Neither money nor appeals to national defense or patriotism will sway him. He aims to protect Anne Savage without doing anything that would give either the Republicans or the Democrats an advantage in the upcoming election, thus preserving his apolitical stance.

He devises a clever but chancy scheme. He tells Savage to purchase fifteen minutes of radio time on the Fourth of July for a speech entitled, "Politics and Ethics: What Every American Should Know," hoping the Democrats, fearing exposure of their blackmail scheme against Savage, will surrender the films. It is a calculated risk because Factor is a tough character who doesn't appear at all frightened by LeVine's ploy and, in fact, taunts him: "All you private dicks are the same: tough talk and bullshit on the outside. Inside, you're a bunch of old ladies." If Factor doesn't back down, then Savage will have to reveal his daughter's participation in stag movies. Neither side budges, and as the time for the broadcast approaches the success of the plan appears doubtful, especially when LeVine and Savage discover that Radio City (where the broadcast will originate) is surrounded by Factor's men, and they might not even be able to get inside the building. A clever bit of disguising allows them to slip into Radio City, and by posing as members of the "Hits and Misses" singing group they are finally able to get into the studio for the broadcast. But with only minutes remaining, there is still no sign of Factor. Finally, with only forty-five seconds to spare, Factor appears and surrenders the films, thus saving Savage from having to make the broadcast. The novel ends with LeVine enjoying a vacation at Savage's Aspen, Colorado, mountain retreat, where he quickly and firmly declines an invitation to join Dewey's campaign. He has done his job well: Anne's reputation remains unscathed; Savage can donate all the money he wishes to Dewey; and no one will be the wiser about Factor's machinations on behalf of FDR. Dewey can go on and get defeated fair and square by FDR in the November election. Bergman is a skillful plotter and by shunning unnecessary complications and distracting subplots, he manages to avoid any annoying and intractable loose ends, a problem that often plagues first novelists, especially in the mystery field. Once the identity of the blackmailers is revealed, the focus of interest is deftly shifted (as it was in Parker's similarly plotted *Mortal Stakes*) to LeVine's problem of how to extricate Savage and his daughter from their dilemma without doing anything that would give either side an advantage in the election. His clever plan provides an imaginative solution to his problem and a most satisfying conclusion to the novel.

Readers interested in mystery novels that deal with important issues, especially political ones, will find *The Big Kiss-Off of 1944* to their liking. It is tempting to read the novel, with its emphasis on the use of political dirty tricks to insure the reelection of the president, as a pointed commentary on the Watergate scandals and subsequent cover-up by Nixon administration figures, but in fact the book was written before the incidents that eventually toppled the Nixon presidency. Thus, Bergman's novel is more prophetic than satiric; for example, Lee Factor's argument that anything is moral if it contributes to the election of the president, and the invocation of "national interest" to justify any action, no matter how immoral or illegal, sound frighteningly similar to defenses offered by any number of Nixon's White House henchmen. In addition, the frantic attempt to cover up the bungled blackmail scheme which, while not apparently involving FDR personally, does involve his trusted aides and military advisors, also parallels Watergate. Bergman's view of American politics, which implies that dedicated but morally obtuse supporters of a political candidate, in this case the President of the United States, will stop at nothing, including blackmail and murder, to insure his reelection, is as cynical as that promulgated by Simon in *The Big Fix*.

Those interested in nostalgia—either for the classic forties detective novel or simply for the past—will find Bergman's re-creation of the forties most skillfully and entertainingly done. The novel is spiced with appropriate slang of the period: expressions like "put the nix on," "tootsie deluxe," "strictly craperoo," "cut the schmooze," "that's jake with me," "fourth-rate palookas," and so forth help create the characteristic sound of the forties. References to popular songs—"Lazy Mary, Will You Get Up?" and "It's Only a Shanty in Old Shantytown"—and movies—James Cagney and Ann Sheridan in *City for Conquest*, Betty Grable in *Pin-Up Girl*, an Esther Williams and Red Skelton comedy—give a sense of the entertainment of the time. America is also at war in 1944, a fact brought home by such moments as LeVine's conversations with a waitress whose son is in the service and with a young mother whose husband is off to war, his despair over the quality of major league baseball as it is being played by wartime's one-armed outfielders and blind, deaf and dumb infielders, and his ration book, which he needs to purchase gasoline. He keeps abreast of current events by listening to H. V. Kaltenborn's newscast on his Stromberg-Carlson radio and even spots Carl Van Doren reading his "World at War" broadcast from Radio City. In evoking the forties, Bergman is not so much interested in satirizing the era as in using it naturally as a backdrop for the action of the novel. Consequently, he takes great care to weave in the many references as unobtrusively as possible in order to create the impression that he is a forties writer, not a seventies writer consciously aping the forties style.

Finally, *The Big Kiss-Off of 1944* can be enjoyed simply for its good writing. Bergman's skillful recapturing of the colorful forties style has already been noted, but equally noteworthy is his ability to create character, to catch the essence of even minor characters in brief, capsulized descriptions, the sort of witty vignette Chandler used so effectively. For example, LeVine describes a desk clerk in a seedy hotel as "a shark-faced man with enough dandruff to fill a pillowcase and eyes that had seen everything and long since stopped caring"; a gas station attendant has "the comic-sad green eyes of a man who hasn't had very much to laugh about, but has retained his sense of humor all the same"; Al Rubine, the two-bit gangster who ends up dead for his blackmailing efforts, is a "small-time crook who found himself in the big time and wanted to get the hell out before he wasn't in any kind of time at all;" Warren Butler, the

homosexual Broadway producer, has "a tinkling laugh like Chinese
bells swaying in the breeze outside a cerise bedroom with lots of
mirrors, a zebra rug, and the most divine four-poster bed."

The hard-boiled detective hero is largely a figure from the past,
a creation of the thirties and forties. In order to present him convincingly in the seventies, contemporary writers like Parker and
Simon have sought to avoid the anachronistic aspects of his character and role by using such strategems as developing his private
life, allowing him complicated personal relationships, placing him
in contemporary situations, and forcing him to deal with topical
issues. Bergman, by contrast, embraces the anachronistic elements
and opts for the past over the present, thus creating in *The Big
Kiss-Off of 1944* a creditable forties-vintage novel. Despite its skillful evocation of the past, however, it transcends nostalgia and parody by dramatizing a serious incident and by creating a hero who is
not only a convincing private detective but an engaging and fully
believable character as well.

HOLLYWOOD AND LeVINE

Hollywood and LeVine (1975) is written in a considerably darker
vein than *The Big Kiss-Off of 1944*, and a comparison between both
novels reveals a shift in emphasis from nostalgia to a more serious
concern with history. In his first novel, Bergman highlighted the
most obvious characteristics of the genre and painted a rich and
lively picture of the forties in order to provide an entertaining context for what was essentially a solid mystery effort. The subject of
political corruption and dirty tricks in the novel was designed to be
taken seriously despite the humor associated with the parodic elements. The situation in *Hollywood and LeVine*—the first stirrings of
the Communist witch hunts in Hollywood in the late forties—is far
more serious, for one thing because it is based on historical fact.
Consequently, the tone, style, and mannerisms of the novel are no

longer aimed at comic effects, as they were in his first novel. Bergman is far more interested in capturing the atmosphere of fear and
intimidation that characterized the period than in evoking nostalgic
echoes of the good old days.

The postwar period was a good one for LeVine. Hired by numerous returning servicemen to check up on their wives, LeVine, a
self-described "private dick with the wise and forgiving heart of a
Talmudic sage," would do nothing for two days, then assure his
clients their wives were girls they could be proud of. Why cripple a
guy's ego and sense of well-being, he argues. Nobody gets hurt,
especially the soldier readjusting to life in the States, and LeVine
earns an easy twenty-five bucks. But by 1947, LeVine's business has
fallen off. The sense of relief at the war's end has faded and optimism is waning perceptively. Then, in February of 1947, everything goes sour for LeVine.

Walter Adrian, successful Hollywood screenwriter (twice nominated for an Academy Award) and former classmate of LeVine's
at City College of New York, pays him a surprise visit. LeVine
hasn't seen Adrian in seven years, but this is obviously not a social
call. Adrian is in trouble. Happily employed by Warner Brothers
for ten years, Adrian explains that now, instead of increasing his
salary to $3500 a week from the $2500 he is currently earning, the
studio is cutting his salary, first offering $2500 a week, then reduc-
ing the figure to $1750. LeVine queries, "They catch you sashaying
around in one of Virginia Mayo's outfits? You shtup someone you're
not supposed to, like Warner's daughter or Minnie Mouse or The
Three Stooges?" But Adrian is in no mood for levity; he is deeply
distressed at what the decrease means—the studio wants him out,
and he claims he doesn't know why. He offers LeVine $300 to come
to California to find out what is going on. The whole thing sounds
suspicious, but for old times sake LeVine agrees to determine what
he can.

Following a thirteen-hour cross-country plane ride, LeVine
arrives in Los Angeles and heads for Adrian's office at Warner
Brothers. Adrian isn't there but has left a note directing LeVine to
the Western street on the back lot, where he is working on a scene.
As LeVine makes his way to the Western street, he passes by a
variety of movie sets—Lower East Side New York, Prohibition
Chicago, Paris, Berlin, Anyville, U.S.A. Suddenly, the fantasy of the

back lot is tragically jolted by reality when he spots the body of Walter Adrian hanging from a rope in the jailhouse on the set. Whatever was worrying him so deeply has driven him to suicide. Or so it appears.

The police are anxious to close the case as quickly as possible. When LeVine suggests to Lieutenant Wynn of the Los Angeles police that Adrian's death might be murder rather than suicide, he replies, "Not if I can help it. There's no evidence of homicide. And thank God for it. Movie industry murders are nothing but trouble. Let's clean this up fast and neat, huh, LeVine?" But LeVine doesn't want to clean it up "fast and neat," especially after having just traveled 3000 miles to help an old friend in trouble. A visit with Adrian's wife, Helen, and a group of friends gathered at her home to mourn his death hints at some dark apprehension. Dale Carpenter, a cowboy actor friend of Adrian's, confesses, "We are worried that Walter was the first victim of something, call it a wave of fear, that's just begun in the last month or so to infect the movie industry." All of Adrian's friends seem affected by the chill in the air, agitated by some unnamed fear. LeVine even finds himself tainted by their paranoia; as he drives away from Adrian's house, he remarks, "I was certain that dozens of eyes were peeking through dozens of curtains."

This unspoken fear is given a name when LeVine learns that Adrian was "as Red as a firetruck" and that, according to Larry Goldmark, his agent, Adrian's brand of politics "is going out of style around Hollywood, like a restaurant with a ptomaine rap, that fast." He adds that there are disturbing rumors of an upcoming congressional investigation of Communism in the movie industry. Lieutenant Wynn tries to convince LeVine that Adrian killed himself because of fears about possible exposure of his Communist activities, and he attempts to dissuade LeVine from pursuing his investigation by producing a secret FBI report on his own political activities (which consist only of signing a petition in 1927 calling for a pardon in the case of Sacco and Vanzetti and contributing to Spanish Refugee Aid in 1938). Undaunted, LeVine refuses to be intimidated and decides to stick with the case until he is satisfied with the explanation. He returns to the jailhouse where Adrian's body was discovered and as he begins nosing around, someone fires several shots at him. Irritated at being shot at, he is nevertheless pleased that his suspicions about Adrian's death are confirmed: "I was working on a flesh-and-blood case, not merely a post-mortem."

Adrian's funeral the next morning draws some of Hollywood's biggest names—John Garfield, Barbara Stanwyck, Humphrey Bogart, Edward G. Robinson, Jack Warner, among others. LeVine is put off by the crass, show business tenor of the service at Temple B'nai Shalom in Beverly Hills, "a ritzy edifice to a sun-tanned God who knew how to look the other way." While Adrian's mother spends the day grieving in a storefront synogogue in Brooklyn, LeVine notes disdainfully that "The God who presided over Beverly Hills—Our Father Who Art in Technicolor—couldn't be bothered with old ladies. This God mingled with the great and blessed their tennis courts and kidney-shaped pools." The young Beverly Hills rabbi even manages to put in a plug for Adrian's final picture by drawing a parallel between the date of its release and Pesach, the release of the Jews from Egypt. LeVine's interest perks up, however, when he hears the eulogies given by some of Adrian's friends, especially that of Henry Perillo, a carpenter and an official in the International Alliance of Theatrical Stage Employees. When Perillo asks, "Is the death of Walter Adrian just the first casualty in a war between the progressive-minded men and women of the movie industry and reactionary lackeys who seek to turn the clock back to the Stone Age?" the gathered assembly begins to shift uncomfortably. He continues:

> Is Walter Adrian . . . the first sacrifice to a clique of reactionary congressmen who hope to fatten themselves off a fearful movie industry, one that thrives on popular acceptance, one whose economic well-being hangs on a slender thread of respectability and imagined 100 percent Americanism? Are the progressive-minded workers of the industry going to hide in their houses and surrender their cherished beliefs in the freedom and dignity of all men, regardless of race or color? I say no! I say Walter Adrian did not die, so that his friends might succumb to an orgy of fear and sterile self-criticism!

Perillo's speech has obviously touched a sensitive nerve, for "an absolutely tubercular explosion of coughing, a violent clearing of a hundred congested throats" follows his comments. When LeVine notices Johnny Parker, Vice-President for production at Warner

Brothers, Adrian's boss and the one responsible for the haggling over his salary, hurriedly leaving the service, he decides to tail him.

He follows Parker's Rolls-Royce from Beverly Hills to a shabby building in a run-down section of Los Angeles. LeVine watches him enter and, shortly afterwards, sees two other men go into the building. One is well-groomed, the other isn't:

> The other guy needed a shave and was attired in a suit of such a peculiar cut that it looked to have the wooden hangers and paper stuffing still inside. He had a curiously baby face behind the growth of beard, with an infant's fatty jowls and the thick eyebrows of an adolescent who had been carpeted with body hair overnight. Most prominent on his pale face was a nose that went down and then abruptly out, like a Rockaway shoot-the-chute. He stood jiggling on the balls of his feet, punching one hand lightly into the other.

LeVine follows them inside and, slipping into the office adjacent to the one which the two men enter, he overhears the man in the ill-fitting suit being introduced to Parker—he is freshman Congressman Richard M. Nixon, who thanks Parker for the effort he is making "to help us crack the hard shell of Communist activity in our great movie industry." LeVine hears Nixon assure Parker that the House Un-American Activities Committee, of which he is a member, will conduct a "sober, responsible investigation of the extent to which the Red shadow has fallen over Hollywood." Nixon also mentions that secret FBI information indicates that Adrian was murdered on orders direct from Moscow to prevent him from giving critical information about the Communist party in Hollywood to the HUAC. Claiming that the facts about Adrian's murder must be kept secret so as not to frighten away other potential witnesses, Nixon argues, all too characteristically, that "The only way to defeat deviousness and guile is to show a little deviousness and guile yourself."

The worst fears of Adrian's friends are confirmed—there apparently will be a full-scale congressional investigation into the influence of Communism in the motion picture industry. However, LeVine doesn't buy Nixon's "cockamaymie" theory that Adrian was murdered by a Moscow agent. When Parker leaves, he follows him to his Beverly Hills home just in time to see Dale Carpenter, the cowboy actor friend of Adrian's, arrive. LeVine gets out of his car and as he is about to move closer to Parker's house, he is hit from behind and knocked out. When he awakens, he finds himself tied to a bed in a seaside cottage and, overhearing his captors' plans for dumping him in the ocean, decides he doesn't like the prospect of becoming "a kosher snack for a slew of sharks." He manages to overpower his two guards and escape to a nearby restaurant, where he phones Helen Adrian, who rescues him, brings him to her house, and soon joins him in the bathtub for a pleasant sexual interlude. However, neither a knock on the head, nor a narrow escape from being fed to the sharks, nor even Helen Adrian's many charms, can dissuade him from getting to the bottom of the situation. He decides he ought to talk with Dale Carpenter right away, but when he reaches his house, he discovers somebody has been there before him. The house is a shambles and Carpenter is sitting by his pool with a couple of bullet holes in his chest. There is no uncertainty about his death—unlike Adrian's death, this cannot be explained away as a suicide.

The following morning, LeVine is hurriedly summoned to Lieutenant Wynn's office, where he is introduced to Congressman Nixon and his companion (whom he recognizes from the meeting with Parker), P. J. Davis, an investigator employed by the HUAC. Davis produces a memo from Clarence White, the chief FBI undercover agent investigating Communist infiltration in Hollywood, informing him that Carpenter, like Adrian, was murdered on orders from Moscow. Nixon, citing "domestic security" (as Lee Factor did on behalf of FDR in *The Big Kiss-Off of 1944* and as Nixon will do twenty-five years later to justify his activities in the White House), attempts to persuade LeVine to cooperate by ending his investigation into Adrian's death. (As they speak, LeVine watches Nixon remove a yellow legal pad from his briefcase and begin taking notes of their conversation because, he explains, "I like to keep a record." This habit of his will, thanks to the more sophisticated electronic taping equipment available in the seventies, prove to be his undoing.) Nixon strongly defends the HUAC:

A great many people from the East—sincere, well-meaning people, I'm sure, . . . seem to think that the House Committee is going to conduct some kind of "witchhunt." Nothing could be further from the truth.

People from the East—and I'm not condemning them, you
understand—many of them say "Oh, these are just a bunch of
politicians looking for headlines, looking for votes." . . . Mr.
LeVine, I wish that were true. I wish it was just something for
headlines, for the papers.

To LeVine, all this "sounded like a bad hashish dream," so he leaves.
Spotting Lemon and Caputo, Wynn's two dim-witted sidekicks, he
discovers it is a relief to stand outside with them: "The two cops
were stupid, but at least they weren't crazy."

The Los Angeles police are cooperating fully with the FBI and
the HUAC to cover up the murders of Adrian and Carpenter but
LeVine, who considers himself just a "private dick checking out a
friend's murder," refuses to go along with their scheme. Although
he can do nothing to alter the fact of Adrian's death, his commitment
to friendship and to the truth compels him to continue investigating.
His only clue, however, is a fragment of an old newspaper he found
at Carpenter's house which refers to the arrest of someone named
James Pardee on a rape charge in Denver. (Newspaper clippings
also conveniently provide key information in both Simon's *Wild
Turkey* and Bergman's *The Big Kiss-Off of 1944*.) An afternoon
spent in the UCLA library poring over old copies of *The Denver
Post* finally yields the rest of the story about Pardee, along with a
photograph which reveals that he is in fact Johnny Parker, now,
sixteen years later, Vice-President of Warner Brothers. Something
else interesting catches his eye. One of the arresting officers is
identified as C. D. White. LeVine wonders if this White could be
the same Clarence White who is now the FBI's master Red-hound
in Hollywood. A check with the Denver police proves he is. LeVine
now knows who was pressuring Parker to squeeze Adrian out of his
Warner Brothers job. If he can find White (who, according to
HUAC investigator Davis, has never been seen by anyone), he
might be able to get some answers about Adrian's death.

LeVine learns from the Denver police that C. D. White left the
force in 1940. When he questions Helen Adrian about her husband's
political friends, he discovers only one—labor organizer Henry
Perillo—came to Hollywood after 1940. Surmising that Perillo might
be Clarence White, he breaks into his house and overhears a phone
conversation which confirms his suspicion. When White finishes

typing a report and leaves the house, LeVine follows him to Warner Brothers studios (where he works as a carpenter) and to the jail-house set where Adrian was found. When he departs, LeVine searches the set and discovers a hidden drawer in a desk which contains the memo White had typed. The memo claims that Helen Adrian is a Russian agent who murdered both her husband and Dale Carpenter. Reading further LeVine is astonished to learn that "New York Party functionary JACOB LEVINE, a 'private detective' operating under the name of 'Jack LeVine' was summoned West to help 'investigate' the death of Adrian" and to create distractions. The memo's conclusion, that Helen Adrian must be allowed to disappear from sight untouched, convinces him that White killed Adrian and Carpenter and is now planning to kill Helen. Having himself been fingered as a Moscow agent, he also knows he is being set up as the prime suspect in the case.

LeVine hurries to the home of the film producer Zach Gross, where he had previously arranged to meet Helen. Gross's party is attended by some of the biggest stars in Hollywood: Katherine Hepburn, Eddie Cantor, Ava Gardner, Gregory Peck, Danny Kaye. Desperately searching for Helen, LeVine manages to step on Spencer Tracy's toe, jostle Paulette Goddard's drink, and rub up against Myrna Loy. But he fails to find Helen. He returns to the parking lot and discovers that White's car, which was parked there when he arrived, is missing, and the attendant informs him that White had just left with a woman matching Helen's description. Finding his own car boxed in between several others, LeVine flags down a blue Cadillac coming up the driveway and asks the driver for help. The man agrees, and tells his companion, Lauren Bacall, to wait for him at the party. LeVine gets in and drives off with Humphrey Bogart in hot pursuit of White and Helen.

What a combination! Jack LeVine, the tough Sunnyside, New York private detective and Humphrey Bogart, filmdom's Sam Spade and Philip Marlowe. Cigarette dangling from his lips, a flask of martinis by his side, Bogart guns his car at speeds up to 120 m.p.h. in pursuit of White. Contemptuous himself of the rumored HUAC hearings ("They'll nail anyone who ever scratched his ass during the National Anthem," he remarks to LeVine), and a friend of the Adrians, he is eager to help LeVine. After a brief delay to change a tire, they eventually catch up with White and in the exciting conclusion to the novel, LeVine, twice wounded in the shoulder, manages to kill White and rescue Helen. Bogart, noticing Levine's wounds, in a fitting gesture of comradeship gives him the shirt off his back to bind his bleeding shoulder.

A final meeting with Lieutenant Wynn clears up the remaining mysteries. Adrian was killed when he went to the jailhouse to block out a scene he was writing and interrupted White in the midst of dropping off a report in the desk hideout. White killed him to protect his cover and then wrote a memo blaming the Communists for the murder. During Adrian's funeral, White's briefcase (which contained the newspaper clipping about Parker's past) got mixed up with Carpenter's, so he had to be killed because he had discovered the link between Parker and White. White intended to kill Helen and then disappear, leaving LeVine to take the blame. However, no one else will ever know the truth about the whole situation. The cover-up has already begun: the FBI denies that Clarence White was ever on its payroll; the Denver police conveniently produce a death certificate for C. D. White; and the death of "Henry Perillo" is attributed to a tragic boating accident.

The novel ends on an ambivalent note. LeVine returns to his beloved New York with Helen Adrian, and the outlook for their future together is promising. However, his final comment to her about the case—"I'd like to think it was just a peculiar set of circumstances, just Hollywood, rather than a preview of things to come. If this Red hunt really gets moving, it'll take years to run out of gas."—is darkly prophetic. For in October, 1947, the House Un-American Activities Committee will open hearings on Communist infiltration of the motion picture industry. Ten witnesses, the famous "Hollywood Ten," will eventually be imprisoned for contempt of court for refusing to answer questions about their political affiliations. The investigation will continue in 1951, and scores of Hollywood figures, including famous actors, actresses, and writers, will be blacklisted for years by the studios. The fear that Adrian and his friends experienced was real, but the situation will turn out to be worse than anything they had imagined. LeVine saves Helen's life, but he can do nothing to prevent the witch hunts that will soon terrorize the Hollywood community.

Bergman effectively re-creates this grim period in American history, but he counts on his reader's awareness of later developments in the investigation for full dramatic impact. In the novel, he depicts a group of people who sense the fear but can only speculate about the future. The reader, knowing the full story about the publicity circus the HUAC hearings turned into, the collusion of the police, the FBI, and other investigators, and the wrenching paranoia that eventually produced Senator Joseph McCarthy, can only shudder helplessly at the portrayal of the preliminaries in *Hollywood and LeVine*.

It is difficult if not impossible to write an historical novel that isn't in some way contaminated by one's contemporary perspective. Rather than adopt a naive view of the past, writers like Bergman use their knowledge (and the reader's knowledge) of history to enhance the resonance of their work. Obviously, Bergman is counting on his reader's awareness of the HUAC investigation of Communism in Hollywood. In addition, the portrait of Nixon, with his chronically suspicious nature, ill-at-ease demeanor, and wooden rhetorical style, depends for its full impact upon the reader's familiarity with the later Nixon, especially the Nixon of the White House years. One can trace a direct relationship between the paranoia and vindictiveness he displays in *Hollywood and LeVine* and his subsequent involvement in the Watergate affair. *The Big Kiss-Off of 1944*, which predated the Watergate incident, achieved a contemporary application only coincidentally. *Hollywood and LeVine*, having been written after the full Watergate story became known, depends upon no such fortuitous circumstance for its telltale portrait of Nixon.

Whereas *The Big Kiss-Off of 1944* shares certain similarities with the detective novel parodies of such writers as Thomas Berger and Richard Brautigan, *Hollywood and LeVine* actually has more in common with a different kind of writing—the intermingling of real and imaginary characters in what might be termed revisionist historical fiction. In Roger Simon's novels, where characters like Howard Eppis, Gunther Thomas, and Jock Hecht are thinly disguised portraits of actual people, one can see a loose approximation of this technique. More to the point, Stuart Kaminsky incorporates many Hollywood celebrities of the forties in his Toby Peters mystery novels (in *Murder On The Yellow Brick Road*, for example, a Munchkin is murdered on the set of *The Wizard of Oz*), mainly for the nostalgic delight of old movie fans. In *Hammett*, mystery writer

Joe Gores re-creates 1928 San Francisco and involves his hero, ex-Pinkerton-agent-turned-writer Dashiell Hammett, in a crime investigation. Like Bergman, Gores imitates a characteristic prose style (Hammett's tough-guy idiom) while at the same time approaching his subject seriously, not in a spirit of either parody or nostalgia.

This effort is not limited to detective writers. In such recent "serious" fiction as E. L. Doctorow's *Ragtime*, Max Apple's *The Oranging of America*, and Robert Coover's *The Public Burning*, brilliantly original effects are achieved by placing real people in imaginative situations: *Ragtime* features Harry Houdini, Henry Ford, and J. Pierpont Morgan; Max Apple's stories include such characters as Howard Johnson, Fidel Castro, Norman Mailer, and Gerald Ford; the most inventive of all is Coover's novel, an outrageous satire about the planned Times Square execution of convicted Soviet spies Julius and Ethel Rosenberg, which employs Richard Nixon as narrator (and as attempted seducer of Ethel Rosenberg). In each of these examples, historical characters and events are depicted from a contemporary point of view, and the comic and satiric effects depend upon the reader's ability to compare the actual with the fictional portraits of the historical personages. Bergman's unique contribution is to combine this revisionist historical approach with the special features of the detective novel to produce an exciting new hybrid form that extends the dimensions of detective fiction into the previously uncharted terrain of the historical novel.

In *Hollywood and LeVine*, Bergman is far less interested in mimicking the jargon and style of the forties detective novel than he was in his first book, although his prose still sparkles with flashes of wit. LeVine, for example, is not above referring to himself as being "every bit as relaxed as a circus aerialist with hemorrhoids," or describing the aroma of a foreign cigarette as being akin "to what you might get off a weight lifter's jockstrap." But for the most part, his colorful similes are less extravagant, more in keeping with the personality Bergman wishes to portray. Thus, many of LeVine's allusions are drawn from the two main interests in his life: poker and baseball. Describing his uneasiness in the case, he says, "It was like sitting down to play poker and discovering that the deck contained sixty cards." He conveys his sympathetic attitude toward Lieutenant Wynn, whose murder investigation is halted by political pressure, by describing him as looking "sour and pensive, like the manager of a sixth-place club in the late innings of the season's last game." LeVine also peppers his wisecracks with baseball references: rejecting the theory that Adrian and Carpenter were murdered on orders from Moscow, he retorts, "I don't see any double knock-off engineered by the Communists, the Red Menace, or Red Ruffing"; lining up a rifle shot, he invokes "the spirits of Jehovah, Zeus, and DiMaggio." The effect of such allusions is to reinforce the image of LeVine as an average guy, a down-to-earth fellow whose interests in such mundane activities as poker and baseball prevent us from seeing him as anything other than a hard-working private detective who happens to find himself mixed up in some very important cases. Although he hobnobs with some of Hollywood's biggest celebrities and is invited to a private meeting with Richard Nixon (and with Thomas Dewey in *The Big Kiss-Off of 1944*), he knows he is just "a small-time shamus" trying to keep his head above water.

LeVine is still bald, and still perspires heavily, but less attention is drawn to these unflattering features in Bergman's second novel. While he isn't miraculously transformed into a handsome leading man once he hits Hollywood, he is obviously attractive enough to land in bed with Helen Adrian, who is, in LeVine's words, "as beautiful as any woman I have ever seen." The plot demands that he become emotionally involved with her so that he will be willing to risk life and limb (and Bogart's life and limb) to rescue her from White at the end. But his intimate relationship with her also allows us to take him more seriously, less the balding, sweating schlemiel who gets diarrhea on a stakeout, more the pretenseless, dedicated professional he really is.

Like Parker and Simon, Bergman is also interested in dramatizing the effects of placing his detective in an unfamiliar setting, but where Parker chose Europe and Simon China, Bergman selects the traditional home of the American private eye, Los Angeles. Here is one area where Bergman works against the convention by showing that Marlowe's and Archer's and Wine's mean streets do not suit LeVine: "Los Angeles. I still had no sense of it, no handle. For two and a half days, I had been wandering through a fun house, losing myself, forgetting my mission for hours at a time." This is nothing more, perhaps, than the native New Yorker's disorientation at first encountering the laid-back, sunshine style of the West Coast.

But LeVine's sense of displacement is real, and is nowhere more strongly felt than when he strolls across the campus of UCLA amidst the tanned muscular men and heartbreaking golden women:

> To a City College dropout like myself, whose classmates had resembled white-skinned, bespectacled frogs, whose experience of co-eds was of an army of dark and large-boned girls already assuming the woeful countenances of their mothers, the spectacle of UCLA was disheartening. I felt old, ugly, and invisible. As I made my way to the library, students seemed to part around me as if stepping past a tree. Why look at a pale yid in a green hat with an army of beach boys to choose from?

By depicting LeVine's uneasiness working in California, Bergman uses the cliché of the Los Angeles private eye to his advantage by differentiating his hero from all those Southern California types who make up the bulk of the private-eye fraternity.

Although his uneasiness in Los Angeles sets him apart from many of his fictional colleagues, his cynical view of the police is identical to theirs. In both *The Big Kiss-Off of 1944* and this novel, the police bow to political pressure and withdraw from important murder investigations. As much as Lieutenant Wynn might like to follow up LeVine's leads about Adrian's death, he succumbs to FBI pressure to cover up the facts. LeVine is interested in the truth about the death of his friend and refuses to abandon his investigation, even at the request of such an important figure as Richard Nixon. As an independent investigator, he is free to follow his own instincts and principles. The police cannot. LeVine also detests their attitudes:

> I loathe cops . . . For sheer calculated rudeness, for pomposity and self-importance, for imbecility, for toadying to superiors and kicking the pants of inferiors, you have to go a long way to beat the officers of the law. In twenty years of private sleuthing, I've had so goddamn many unpleasant, underhanded, and depressing encounters with homicide dicks and robbery squads that I'm beyond the point of retrieval.

Although he exempts certain individual officers from his scorn, he unequivocally rejects, as do most of his colleagues, the police in general for their inadequacies, especially for their lack of commitment to truth and justice.

Hollywood and LeVine represents a distinct movement away from nostalgia and parody toward hard-nosed realism; in many ways, the book is a history novel masquerading as a mystery, with Bergman doing a skillful job of evoking the atmosphere of fear and intimidation that led to the Hollywood witch hunts of the forties and fifties. But in addition to being a vivid and authentic re-creation of history, *Hollywood and LeVine* is also an excellent novel: the plot is tightly organized and skillfully developed; each scene is integral to the overall design of the book; the characters, both real and imaginary, are realistically portrayed; the style is colorful and polished. Bergman has managed to accomplish what so many of his fellow writers in the genre have attempted, often with less success—the combination of a ripping good mystery with a pointed commentary on social and political issues. *Hollywood and LeVine* is both a first-rate mystery novel and one of the best fictional accounts ever written about this bleak period in American history. Its remarkable success provides yet another convincing example of how—in the talented hands of such writers a Robert Parker, Roger Simon, and Andrew Bergman—the dimensions of the hard-boiled novel are continually being extended into fresh and exciting new areas.

Notes

1. Robert B. Parker

"of his youth" — Letter to author, 30 October 1978.

"own private detective" — Ibid.

"at without result" — Joan H. Parker and Robert B. Parker, *Three Weeks in Spring* (Boston: Houghton Mifflin, 1978), p. 135.

"as it came" — Ibid., p. 56.

"what we fear" — Ibid., p. 40.

"his detective hero" — Letter to author.

THE GODWULF MANUSCRIPT

"in the air" — Robert B. Parker, *The Godwulf Manuscript* (1974; rpt. New York: Berkley Medallion, 1975), p. 70. All subsequent quotes are from this edition. (Houghton Mifflin is the original publisher of all of Parker's novels.)

"settled on Spenser" — Letter to author, 30 October 1978.

"but the detective" — Robert B. Parker, "The Violent Hero, Wilderness Heritage and Urban Reality: A Study of the Private Eye in the Novels of Dashiell Hammett, Raymond Chandler and Ross Macdonald" (Unpublished doctoral dissertation, Boston University, 1970), p. 8.

PAGE	QUOTE	SOURCE

"be really trying" — Raymond Chandler, *The Big Sleep* (1939; rpt. New York: Ballantine Books, 1971), p. 1. First published in New York by Alfred A. Knopf.

"before I sleep" — Robert Frost, *The Complete Poems of Robert Frost* (New York: Holt, Rinehart and Winston, 1964), p. 275.

"they have married" — Philip Durham, *Down These Mean Streets a Man Must Go* (Chapel Hill, North Carolina: The University of North Carolina Press, 1963), p. 92.

GOD SAVE THE CHILD

"It was resonant" — Robert B. Parker, *God Save the Child* (1974; rpt. New York: Berkley Medallion, 1976), p. 24. All subsequent quotes are from this edition.

"parent and child" — Parker, "The Violent Hero," p. 150.

"neon-lighted slum either" — Raymond Chandler, *The Little Sister* (1949; rpt. New York: Ballantine Books, 1971), p. 202. First published in Boston by Houghton Mifflin.

"awesome as creation" — Ross Macdonald, *The Instant Enemy* (1968; rpt. New York: Bantam, 1969), p. 1.

"the endless city" — Ross Macdonald, *Sleeping Beauty* (1973; rpt. New York: Bantam, 1974), p. 75. Both Macdonald books were first published in New York by Alfred A. Knopf.

MORTAL STAKES

"in each case" — Dorothy Gardiner and Katherine Sorley Walker, eds., *Raymond Chandler Speaking* (Boston: Houghton Mifflin, 1962), p. 222.

"Pimp is in" — Robert B. Parker, *Mortal Stakes* (1975; rpt. New York: Berkley Medallion, 1977), p. 81. All subsequent quotes are from this edition.

"and the future's sakes" — Frost, *Complete Poems* p. 359.

"killer of men" — Parker, "The Violent Hero," p. 104.

PAGE	QUOTE	SOURCE

PROMISED LAND

"they were saps"
Robert B. Parker, *Promised Land* (1976; rpt. New York: Berkley Medallion, 1978), p. 131. All subsequent quotes are from this edition.

"romance, however passionate"
W. H. Auden, *A Certain World: A Commonplace Book* (New York: The Viking Press, 1970), p. 248.

"one fine morning"
F. Scott Fitzgerald, *The Great Gatsby* (New York: Scribner's, 1925), p. 159.

THE JUDAS GOAT

"what I need"
Robert B. Parker, *The Judas Goat* (Boston: Houghton Mifflin, 1978), p. 5. All subsequent quotes are from this edition.

Slotkin argues
Richard Slotkin, *Regeneration Through Violence: The Mythology of the American Frontier, 1600–1860* (Middletown, Conn: Wesleyan University Press, 1973), pp. 6–24.

"his private life"
Parker "The Violent Hero," p. 81.

2.   Roger L. Simon

"fiction in years"
Roger L. Simon, *The Big Fix* (1973; rpt. New York: Pocket Books, 1974). First published in San Francisco by Straight Arrow Press.

"wonderful prose" and subsequent quotes
Telephone conversation with Roger Simon, 13 February 1979.

"consciousness to revolution."
Roger L. Simon, *The Mama Tass Manifesto* (New York: Holt, Rinehart and Winston, 1970), p. 69.

"of American society"
Ibid., p. 21.

THE BIG FIX

"of the rich"
Leslie Fiedler, *Love and Death in the American Novel*, Revised Ed. (New York: Stein and Day, 1966), p. 499.

"dodgers as admirers"
Roger L. Simon, *The Big Fix* (1973; rpt. New York: Pocket Books, 1974), p. 79. All subsequent quotes are from this edition.

WILD TURKEY

"shirt and jeans"   Roger L. Simon, *Wild Turkey* (1975; rpt.
                         New York: Pocket Books, 1976), p. 18.
                         All subsequent quotes are from this edi-
                         tion. First published in San Francisco by
                         Straight Arrow Press.

PEKING DUCK

"your automobile   Roger L. Simon, *Peking Duck* (New
registration"   York: Simon and Schuster, 1979), p. 13.
                         All subsequent quotes are from this
                         edition.

3.   Andrew Bergman

"went berserk" and   Telephone conversation with Andrew
subsequent quotes   Bergman, 11 April 1979.

THE BIG KISS-OFF OF 1944

"on the rug"   Andrew Bergman, *The Big Kiss-Off of
                         1944* (1974; rpt. New York: Ballantine
                         Books, 1975), p. 66. All subsequent quotes
                         are from this edition. First published in
                         New York by Holt, Rinehart and Winston.

HOLLYWOOD AND LEVINE

"a Talmudic sage"   Andrew Bergman, *Hollywood and LeVine*
                         (New York: Holt, Rinehart and Winston,
                         1975), p. 2. All subsequent quotes are
                         from this edition.

Bibliography

I. Works by Robert B. Parker

A. NOVELS

The Godwulf Manuscript. Boston: Houghton Mifflin, 1974; rpt. New York: Berkley Medallion, 1975.

God Save the Child. Boston: Houghton Mifflin, 1974; rpt. New York: Berkley Medallion, 1976.

Mortal Stakes. Boston: Houghton Mifflin, 1975; rpt. New York: Berkley Medallion, 1977.

Promised Land. Boston: Houghton Mifflin, 1976; rpt. New York: Berkley Medallion, 1978.

The Judas Goat. Boston: Houghton Mifflin, 1978; rpt. New York: Berkley Medallion, 1979.

B. OTHER WORKS

"The Grim Laughter: Hamlet and the Renaissance." *Lock Haven Review* 12 (1971): 81–89.

"Marxism and the Mystery." In *Murder Ink: The Mystery Reader's Companion*, edited by Dilys Winn. New York: Workman Publishing, 1977, pp. 123–25.

"The Prince and the King: Shakespeare's Machiavellian Cycle." *Revue des Langues Vivantes*, Fall 1970.

"The Violent Hero, Wilderness Heritage and Urban Reality: A Study of the Private Eye in the Novels of Dashiell Hammett, Raymond Chandler and Ross Macdonald." Unpublished doctoral dissertation, Boston University, 1970.

[Parker] and Peter Sandberg, eds. *Order and Diversity*. New York: John Wiley Co., 1973. Textbook.

[Parker], DeLisle, Ridlon, and Yokelson, eds. *The Personal Response to Literature*. Boston: Houghton Mifflin, 1971. Textbook.

With John R. Marsh. *Sports Illustrated Training With Weights*. Philadelphia: J. B. Lippincott, 1974.

With Joan H. Parker. *Three Weeks in Spring*. Boston: Houghton Mifflin, 1978.

II. Works About Robert B. Parker

A. SELECTED REVIEWS, LISTED CHRONOLOGICALLY

Callendar, Newgate. Review of *The Godwulf Manuscript*. *New York Times Book Review*, 13 January 1974, p. 12.

———. Review of *God Save the Child*. *New York Times Book Review*, 5 December 1974, p. 10.

Duffy, Martha. Review of *God Save the Child*. *Time*, 10 February 1975, p. 76.

Callendar, Newgate. Review of *Mortal Stakes*. *New York Times Book Review*, 4 January 1976, p. 22.

Winks, Robin. Review of *Promised Land*. *New Republic*, 16 October 1976, p. 30.

Callendar, Newgate. Review of *Promised Land*. *New York Times Book Review*, 31 October 1976, p. 40.

Binyon, T. J. Review of *Mortal Stakes*. *Times Literary Supplement*, 12 November 1976, p. 1437.

Winks, Robin. Review of *Mortal Stakes*. *New Republic*, 19 March 1977, p. 35.

———. Review of *The Judas Goat*. *New Republic*, 4 November 1978, p. 53.

Demarest, Michael. Review of *The Judas Goat*. *Time*, 20 November 1978, p. 118.

Callendar, Newgate. Review of *The Judas Goat*. *New York Times Book Review*, 17 December 1978, p. 28.

I. Works by Roger L. Simon

A. NOVELS

Heir. New York: The Macmillan Co., 1968.

The Mama Tass Manifesto. New York: Holt, Rinehart and Winston, 1970.

The Big Fix. San Francisco: Straight Arrow Books, 1973; rpt. New York: Pocket Books, 1974.

Wild Turkey. San Francisco: Straight Arrow Books, 1975; rpt. New York: Pocket Books, 1976.

Peking Duck. New York: Simon and Schuster, 1979.

B. OTHER WORKS

The Big Fix. Universal Studios, 1978. Screenplay.

II. Works About Roger L. Simon

A. SELECTED REVIEWS, LISTED CHRONOLOGICALLY

Prescott, Peter. Review of *The Big Fix*. *Newsweek*, 16 July 1973, p. 88.

Callendar, Newgate. Review of *The Big Fix*. *New York Times Book Review*, 14 April 1974, p. 14.

Hamilton-Paterson, James. Review of *The Big Fix*. *Times Literary Supplement*, 10 January 1975, p. 29.

Callendar, Newgate. Review of *Wild Turkey*. *New York Times Book Review*, 6 July 1975, p. 14.

Davies, Russell. Review of *Wild Turkey*. *Times Literary Supplement*, 18 June 1976, p. 732.

Callendar, Newgate. Review of *Peking Duck*. *New York Times Book Review*, 22 July 1979, p. 16.

I. Works by Andrew Bergman

A. NOVELS

The Big Kiss-Off of 1944. New York: Holt, Rinehart and Winston, 1974; rpt. New York: Ballantine Books, 1975.

Hollywood and LeVine. New York: Holt, Rinehart and Winston, 1975.

B. OTHER WORKS

We're In the Money: Depression America and Its Films. New York: New York University Press, 1971.

James Cagney. New York: Galahad Books, 1973.

With Mel Brooks, Norman Steinberg, Richard Pryor, and Alan Uger. *Blazing Saddles*. Warner Brothers, 1974. Screenplay.

The In-Laws. Warner Brothers, 1979. Screenplay.

II.   Works About Andrew Bergman

A.   SELECTED REVIEWS, LISTED CHRONOLOGICALLY

Callendar, Newgate. Review of *The Big Kiss-Off of 1944*. *New York Times Book Review*, 31 March 1974, p. 41.

Davies, Russell. Review of *The Big Kiss-Off of 1944*. *Times Literary Supplement*, 7 March 1975, p. 241.

Lingeman, Richard. Review of *Hollywood and LeVine*. *New York Times*, 4 September 1975, p. 33.

Callendar, Newgate. Review of *Hollywood and LeVine*. *New York Times Book Review*, 7 September 1975, p. 39.

Binyon, T. J. Review of *Hollywood and LeVine*. *Times Literary Supplement*, 6 August 1976, p. 998.

Miscellaneous

Binyon, T. J. "A Lasting Influence?" In *The World of Raymond Chandler*, edited by Miriam Ross. New York: A & W Publishers, 1977, p. 182. (Comments on Parker and Bergman)

Geherin, David. "The Hard-Boiled Detective Hero in the 1970's: Some New Candidates." *The Armchair Detective*, January 1978, pp. 49–51.

Index